Cloudless Sky

His Eminence the Third Jamgön Kongtrül Rinpoche

CLOUDLESS
SKY
The Mahamudra Path of the Tibetan Kagyü Buddhist School

THE THIRD JAMGÖN KONGTRÜL

......

Edited and translated from Tibetan into German by
TINA DRASCZYK AND ALEX DRASCZYK

English translation by
RICHARD GRAVEL

SHAMBHALA
Boston & London
1992

SHAMBHALA PUBLICATIONS, INC.
Horticultural Hall
300 Massachusetts Avenue
Boston, Massachusetts 02115
www.shambhala.com

The Nālandā Translation Committee translation of "The Vajra Song of the First Jamgön Kongtrül Rinpoche" is taken from *The Rain of Wisdom* (Boston: Shambhala Publications, 1980, 1989), in which the song is entitled "The Song of Lodrö Thaye." "The Supplication to the Kagyü Gurus" is taken from the same source. Both are copyright © 1980 by Chögyam Trungpa and reprinted with the permission of the Nālandā Translation Committee, 1619 Edward Street, Halifax, Nova Scotia, Canada B3H 3H9.

Printed in the United States of America

Distributed in the United States by Random House, Inc.,
and in Canada by Random House of Canada Ltd

LIBRARY OF CONGRESS CATALOGING-IN-PUBLICATION DATA

Kongtrul, Jamgon, 1954–
    Cloudless sky: the Mahamudra path of the Tibetan Kagyu Buddhist School /
Jamgon Kongtrul; edited and translated from Tibetan into German by
Tina Drasczyk and Alez Drasczyk; English translation by Richard Gravel.
    p. cm.
    Includes bibiographical references.
    ISBN 0-87773-694-4
    ISBN 1-57062-604-9
    1. Mahāmudrā (Tantric rite). 2. Meditation—Bka'-rgyud-pa (Sect).
    I. Drasczyk, Tina. II. Drasczyk, Alex. III. Title.
BQ7679.6.K66 1992   92-50119
294.3'443—dc20   CIP

Frontispiece photo: Blair Hansen
BVG 01

*Dedicated to His Holiness
the Seventeenth Gyalwa Karmapa*

Contents

......

Foreword

......

During the October 1987 visit of His Eminence Jamgön Kongtrül Rinpoche to various Kagyü centers in Austria, a seminar was held in the mountains near Salzburg. The subject of the seminar was a vajra song which originally had been sung by Lodrö Thaye, the first Jamgön Kongtrül Rinpoche, as a spontaneous expression of mahamudra experience. This song is part of the *Kagyü Gurtso,* the "Ocean of Songs of the Kagyüs." Using the vajra song as a starting point, H. E. Jamgön Kongtrül Rinpoche presented both an overview of mahamudra, the heart of the Kagyü teachings, and some very practical advice for those who wish to tread upon the mahamudra path.

In view of the interest expressed by a great number of people in obtaining these instructions, we consulted H. E. Jamgön Kongtrül Rinpoche and decided to publish the talks in the form of a book in order to provide insight into the treasury of mahamudra teachings and their unbroken transmission by the Kagyü lineage. It is important to stress, however, that the actual practice of mahamudra requires oral instructions from a teacher who is part of an authentic transmission lineage.

Finally, we would like to express our heartfelt thanks to H. E. Jamgön Kongtrül Rinpoche for the teachings contained in this book and for his boundless activity. In addition, we would like to thank everyone who has contributed to the preparation of this book.

By the inspiration of the Kagyü lineage, may the realization of mahamudra be speedily accomplished. May all beings enjoy the happiness they long for.

Tina Drasczyk and Alex Drasczyk

Preface

· · · · ·

When receiving or reading teachings it is important always to maintain a completely pure inner attitude. In this regard, there are three errors to be avoided, which can be likened to three types of vessels.

The first error is not paying attention; this is like an upside-down vessel, into which no liquid can be poured. The second error is not committing the meaning to memory; this is like a vessel with a hole in the bottom, which cannot retain the liquid poured into it. The third error is being distracted by conflicting emotions; this is like a vessel containing poison, which will contaminate the liquid.

One should strive to be free from these errors and cultivate the pure attitude of bodhichitta, the mind of enlightenment.

Jamgön Kongtrül Rinpoche

Cloudless Sky

The Vajra Song of the
First Jamgön Kongtrül Rinpoche

......

The illustrious one, Vajradhara,
Who is said to possess the eight good qualities,
Is seen in human form by ordinary men like us.
You are the refuge called Padma, endowed with blessings.
From the eight-petaled lotus dome of my heart,
I supplicated you not to be separate even for an instant.
Though I did not have the good fortune of realization and
    liberation at once,
I was blessed with just recognizing my own nature.

Therefore, concern for the eight worldly dharmas
    diminished,
And I clearly saw the famous luminous dharmakaya
By mixing my mind with the guru's.
I discovered nonthought in the midst of discursive
    thought,
And within nonconcept, wisdom dawned.
Now, with the joyous appreciation of a lineage son of the
    Takpo buddha,
I am inspired to speak out.

In the west, in Uddiyana, the secret treasure ground of the
    dakinis,

The great siddha Tilo
Opened the treasure of the three gems.

In the north, in the hermitage of Ravishing Beautiful
    Flowers,
The learned Mahapandita Naro
Showed the mark of a siddha, indivisible prana and mind.

In the south, in the land of herbs, the valley of Trowo,
The translator, emanated from Hevajra,
Established the source of the river of all siddhas.

In the west, in the Lachi snow range,
The supreme being, Shepa Dorje,
Attained the state of unity in one lifetime.

In the east, in heavenly Taklha Gampo,
The honorable physician, the second victorious one,
Realized the samadhi of the tenth bhumi.

In the chakras of body, speech, and mind,
The host of siddhas of the four great and eight lesser
    lineages
Obtained the life-force of mahamudra
And could not help but attain enlightenment.
Skilled in magnetizing through bodhichitta,
They could not help but benefit beings.
Having obtained the profound wealth, the perfection of
    the two accumulations,
They could not help but become prosperous.
Fully understanding that knowing one liberates all,
They could not help but fulfill the great prophecy.

Lineage sons of these wealthy fathers
Possess the great self-existing riches of this previous
    karma.

They are the children of snow lionesses and great garudas.
By the power of their family bloodline, they are completely
   mature at once.
As followers of the lineage of Kagyü siddhas,
Their meditation is naturally born through the power of
   these blessings.

Bragging of their pain in many years of practice,
Proud of dwelling in indolence,
Boasting of having endured such pain,
Undermining others and haughty,
Keeping score with discursive thoughts of self and others
In counting up the realizations of the bhumis and the
   paths,
These are the qualities of the ignorant meditators in this
   dark age.
We do not possess these, and though I do not have the title
   of a siddha,
Nevertheless, through the excellent oral instructions of the
   example lineage,
I have seen the wisdom of ultimate mahamudra.

Ground mahamudra is the view, understanding things as
   they are.
Path mahamudra is the experience of meditation.
Frutition mahamudra is the realization of one's mind as
   buddha.
I am unworthy, but my guru is good.
Though born in the dark age, I am very fortunate.
Though I have little perseverance, the oral instructions are
   profound.

······

As for ground mahamudra:
There are both things as they are and the way of confusion.

It does not incline toward either samsara of nirvana,
And is free from the extremes of exaggeration and
    denigration.
Not produced by causes, not changed by conditions,
It is not spoiled by confusion
Nor exalted by realization.
It does not know either confusion or liberation.

Since no essence exists anywhere,
Its expression is completely unobstructed and manifests
    everything.
Pervading all of samsara and nirvana like space,
It is the ground of all confusion and liberation,
With its self-luminous consciousness
And its alaya-vijñana.
As for the cognitive aspect of this neutral state,
Its essence is empty and its nature is luminous.
These two are inseparable and are the quintessence of
    insight.
It is space, ungraspable as a thing.
It is a spotless precious clear crystal.
It is the glow of the lamp of self-luminous mind.
It is inexpressible, the experience of a mute.
It is unobscured, transparent wisdom,
The luminous dharmakaya, sugatagarbha,
Primordially pure and spontaneous.
It cannot be shown through analogy by anyone,
And it cannot be expressed in words.
It is the dharmadhatu, which overwhelms mind's
    inspection.

Established in this to begin with,
One should cut all doubts.
When one practices meditation with the view,

It is like a garuda fathoming space.
There is no fear and no doubt.
The one who meditates without the view
Is like a blind man wandering the plains.
There is no reference point for where the true path is.
The one who does not meditate, but merely holds the view
Is like a rich man tethered by stinginess.
He is unable to bring appropriate fruition to himself and
      others.
Joining the view and meditation is the holy tradition.

As for the ignorant aspect of this neutral state,
One does not know one's nature because of the five causes.
In the ocean of coemergent ignorance,
The waves of ego-fixation's confusion roll.
Cognition becomes a self, and projections become objects,
And so the habitual patterns of grasping and fixation
      solidify.
Thus, karma accumulates and then fully ripens.
The rim of the waterwheel of samsara turns,
But even while it turns, its essence is unstained.
Even while it appears, it is empty of reality.
Mere appearance is the vividness of the trikaya.
Unborn is the nature of birth;
That unborn is unceasing.
On the threshold of nonduality, there is nowhere to dwell.
From this mind, difficult to express,
Various magical displays of samsara and nirvana arise.
Recognizing these as self-liberated is the supreme view.
When this is realized, everything is suchness.
When there are no obstructions or attainments, this is the
      innate nature.
When conceptual mind is transcended, this is the ultimate.

······

As for path mahamudra:
Mind and the phenomenal world are mahamudra.
Coemergent mind is dharmakaya.
Coemergent appearance is the light of dharmakaya.
When the blessings of the glorious guru
And one's karma come together,
One realizes one's nature like meeting an old friend.

There is no point in much talk,
But the beginner needs various things.
One should abandon either welcoming or sending off
	thoughts of past and future.
The instantaneous mind of nowness
Is the unfabricated innate nature.
In meditation, there should be no trace of deliberateness.
One should not stray for an instant in confusion.
Nonwandering, nonmeditation, nonfabrication are the
	point.
With freshness, looseness, and clarity,
In the space of the three gates of liberation,
One is mindful, establishing proper watchfulness.
Always keeping the mind balanced between tight and
	relaxed,
One pacifies the accumulation of subtle, tangible, and
	gross thoughts.
Rest in the state of natural, unfabricated mind.

The four levels of experiences arise in succession,
And the sun of luminosity continually dawns.
The root of mahamudra meditation is established.
Without it, one's talk of higher realization
Is like building a house without a foundation.

However, excessive desire for this is the work of Mara.
Those who persevere but have little learning
Are deceived by superficial virtues
And lead themselves and others along the way to the lower
    realms.
Even the good experiences of bliss, luminosity, and
    nonthought
Are the cause of samsara if one fixates on them.

When you intensify devotion in your heart,
Rock meets bone in insight,
And the ultimate lineage blessing is received.
Not straying into the four strayings,
Not falling into the three misunderstandings,
Transcending the four joys, free from the three conditions,
Realizing through the three stages of birth,
Untouched by the mind of the three great ones,
This is the self-existing nature, undefiled by experience.

Like the center of a cloudless sky,
The self-luminous mind is impossible to express.
It is wisdom of nonthought beyond analogy,
Naked ordinary mind.
Not keeping to dogmatism or arrogance,
It is clearly seen as dharmakaya.
The appearance of the six sense objects, like the moon in
    water,
Shines in the state of wisdom.
Whatever arises is the unfabricated innate state.
Whatever appears is the nature of mahamudra.
The phenomenal world is dharmakaya great bliss.

Both shamatha meditation of natural resting
And vipashyana, which sees the unseeable,

Should not be separated but unified
In stillness, occurrence, and awareness.
Beyond abandoning discursive confusion,
Beyond applying antidotes,
There will be a time when you spontaneously reach this.

When you have achieved realization,
There is nothing other than the meditative state.
At the threshold of freedom from loss and gain,
Even meditation does not exist.
But for those beginners who are unable to dissolve the
        hairline of conceptualization,
Meditation is important.
When one practices meditation, there is experience.
This experience arises as the adornment of insight.

This path is divided into the four yogas:
One-pointedness means recognizing the nature of mind;
Divided into the lesser, medium, and greater stages:
One sees the alternation of bliss and luminosity,
One masters resting in samadhi,
And experience continuously appears as luminosity.

Simplicity means realizing the mind is without root;
Divided into the lesser, medium, and greater stages:
One realizes that the arising, ceasing, and dwelling are
        empty,
One is free from the ground and root of fixating on
        appearance or emptiness,
And one resolves the complexity of all dharmas.

One taste means dissolving appearance and mind into each
        other;
Divided into the lesser, medium, and greater stages:

All dharmas of samsara and nirvana are dissolved into
    equal taste,
Appearance and mind become like water poured into
    water,
And from one taste, the various wisdoms arise.

Nonmeditation means the utter exhaustion of conceptual
    mind;
Divided into the lesser, medium, and greater stages:
One is free from meditation and meditator,
The habitual patterns of primitive beliefs about reality are
    gradually cleared away,
And the mother and son luminosity dissolve together.
The wisdom of dharmadhatu extends throughout space.

In short, in meditation:
One-pointedness means that mind is still as long as one
    wishes,
Seeing the very nature of ordinary mind.
Simplicity means the realization of groundlessness.
One taste means liberating
All possible dualistic fixations through insight.
Nonmeditation means transcending all sophistries of
    meditation and nonmeditation,
The exhaustion of habitual patterns.

In this way, from the great lords of yogins,
Naropa and Maitripa,
Down to the lord guru Padma Wangchen,
The golden garland of the Kagyüs
Reached the dharmakaya kingdom of nonmeditation,
Spontaneously cleared away the darkness of the two
    obscurations,
Expanded the great power of the two knowledges,

Opened the treasury of benefit for the sake of others
    pervading space,
And remained in the refuge of mind free from doubt.
The Kagyü lineage is known to be passed from one to
    another.
It is known not by words alone, but by their meaning.
Please guide even such a lowborn savage as myself,
Who possesses the merest mark of your noble lineage,
Quickly to the kingdom of nonmeditation.
Kind one, please utterly exhaust my conceptual mind.

······

The fruition mahamudra is spoken of like this:
The ground is receiving the transmission of the innate
    trikaya;
The path is applying the key points of the view and
    meditation;
The fruition is the actualization of the stainless trikaya.
Therefore, its essence is emptiness, simplicity, dharmakaya.
Its manifestation is the luminous nature of sambhogakaya.
Its strength, manifold and unceasing, is nirmanakaya.
This is the sovereign of all reality.
The nature of mahamudra is unity,
The realm of dharmas free from accepting or rejecting.
Possessing the beauty of unconditioned bliss,
It is the great and vast wealth of wisdom.
It is the natural form of kindness transcending thought.
Through prajña, it does not dwell in samsara.
Through karuna, it does not dwell in nirvana.
Through effortlessness, buddha activity is spontaneously
    accomplished.
The luminosity of ground and path, mother and son,
    dissolve together.

The ground and fruition embrace one another.
Buddha is discovered in one's mind.
The wish-fulfilling treasure overflows within.
E ma! How wonderful and marvelous!

Since in the view of mahamudra
Analysis does not apply,
Cast mind-made knowledge far away.
Since in the meditation of mahamudra
There is no way of fixating on a thought,
Abandon deliberate meditation.
Since in the action of mahamudra
There is no reference point for any action,
Be free from the intention to act or not.
Since in the fruition of mahamudra
There is no attainment to newly acquire,
Cast hopes, fears, and desires far away.

This is the depth of the mind of all Kagyüs.
It is the only path on which the victorious ones and their
        sons journey.
Theirs is the upaya that reverses the vicious circle of
        existence
And the dharma that brings enlightenment in one life.
Here is the essence of all the teachings, sutras, and tantras.
May I and all sentient beings pervading space
Together attain the simultaneity of realization and
        liberation,
And attain supreme mahamudra.

In order not to transgress the command seal of emptiness
endowed with all the supreme aspects, the one whose
knowledge is transcendent and who manifested in the form

of the vajraholder, I, the subject of Padma, the Yönten Gyatso Lodrö Thaye, composed this at Künzang Dechen Ösal Ling on the left slope of the third Devikoti, Tsari-like Jewel Rock. SHUBHAM

Commentary by the
Third Jamgön Kongtrül Rinpoche
......

INTRODUCTION

The mahasiddhas of India often expressed their insights in the form of songs, known as dohas, or vajra songs. This tradition was continued in Tibet by the masters of the Kagyü transmission. One very well-known collection of such songs is the *Kagyü Gurtso,* or "Ocean of Kagyü Songs."

Buddha Shakyamuni gave countless teachings in which he described different paths. The goal of these teachings is to achieve insight into ultimate truth, which is the nature of our minds. Of all the approaches taught by the Buddha, mahamudra is considered the most excellent. This was the approach followed by the early teachers of the Kagyü tradition, who achieved complete realization within a single lifetime, relying exclusively on the path of mahamudra and its skillful means.

Fortunately, the early teachers did not keep their insights to themselves but expressed them in the form of songs. These songs are in fact not ordinary songs of the kind that can be written or composed. They arise neither from a particular cause nor for a particular purpose. The extraordinary aspect of these songs is that they spontaneously express inner experiences and transmit the complete meaning of mahamudra and all its aspects—view, action, and meditation. They deal with the ultimate teachings presented by the perfect Buddha, the teachings about ultimate truth. This is why these dohas are described as vajra dohas, because their meaning is indestructible and unchanging.

The vajra songs of the Kagyü Gurtso date back to the earlier Kagyü masters. When reciting them today, we should adjust our body, speech, and mind so as to take full advantage of the recitation. With regard to the body, one should wear appropriate clothing, for instance the three dharma robes if one has taken the vows. With regard to speech, one should sing the melody with great accuracy and pronounce each word properly. Mentally, one should concentrate on every word and internalize its meaning. In this way, one should not simply recite the text but should take great care to involve one's body, speech, and mind in reading the vajra song.

Vajra songs are meant to help the practitioner overcome three types of obstacles: outer, inner (disturbances related to prana, nadi, and bindu), and secret (those that interfere with spiritual progress and meditation). The practice of mahamudra, the way of the Kagyüs, is based mainly on trust and surrender. By reading the vajra songs, one not only develops the three types of trust—the trust of conviction, the trust of longing, and pure trust—but also learns to surrender. By keeping the examples of one's teachers in mind, one achieves the inner certainty that it is possible to follow the path and, through one's practice, attain realization.

In addition, as mentioned above, each vajra song contains the entire meaning of the teachings of Buddha: emptiness, codependent origination, precious bodhichitta, and insight into the unity of emptiness and compassion; one taste, the unity of samsara and nirvana; impermanence, the constant transformation of all things; and many other teachings. This means that if one actually manages to understand and transplant within oneself the meaning of the song, then one is not only directing one's body, speech, and mind toward the dharma, but is also treading the path itself and giving rise to limitless benefits.

The essence of the countless teachings of Buddha is the explanation of buddha-nature, the luminosity that abides in the mind of every single being. As long as one does not recognize one's buddha-nature, one experiences the confusion of samsara. However, realizing the potential of buddhahood that lies within is in itself buddhahood. Buddha's instructions were basically methods to help one overcome confusion and recognize the true nature of mind. The teachings of mahamudra, known as the "path of liberation," represent the pinnacle of the Buddha's teachings.

What is meant by mahamudra? Mahamudra consists basically of three aspects: ground, path, and view mahamudra. Ground mahamudra is the unity of relative truth and ultimate truth. It is freedom from both the two extremes of eternalism, or belief in lasting and true existence, and nihilism, or belief in the nonexistence of phenomena.

Path mahamudra is the union of skillful means and wisdom. But not falling into the extremes of either nihilism or the belief in the permanence of appearances, and by not neglecting either wisdom or skillful means, one accomplishes the two types of accumulations. These are the accumulation of object-related merit and the accumulation of nonreferential wisdom. In essence, the path consists in uniting these two accumulations.

Fruition mahamudra is freedom from the extremes of samsara and nirvana. It is based on ground mahamudra, the unity of relative and ultimate truths, and on path mahamudra, the unity of the two accumulations. In this state, there is no difference between the three realms of samsara and liberation or nirvana. Fruition mahamudra is the realization of the unity of dharmakaya and the form kayas.

Since mahamudra encompasses the three aspects of ground, path, and fruition, it should be evident that there is nothing that it does not accommodate. It includes everything, from the state of confusion concerning the nature of the path up to the realization of perfect buddhahood. In other words, mahamudra is recognizing the nature of one's own mind.

The Tibetan word for mahamudra is *chak gya chenpo.* *Chak* refers to emptiness which is perfect in every respect; *gya chenpo,* the great expanse, refers to the all-encompassing wisdom inherent in emptiness. The meaning of this gloss is that in its depth and breadth, mahamudra encompasses everything. Mahamudra is the "path of liberation," the highest of all paths, the quickest and most profound way to buddhahood. He who was foretold by the Victorious One in the *Samadhirajasutra* and elsewhere, the glorious, holy guru Lodrö Thaye, also called Karma Ngakwang Yönten Gyatso,[1] composed this vajra doha having accomplished the realization of mahamudra. It is entitled "The Self-Arising Innate Song upon Acquiring a Mere Glimpse of Certainty in the View and Meditation of the Incomparable Takpo Kagyü."

The illustrious one, Vajradhara,
Who is said to possess the eight good qualities,[2]
Is seen in human form by ordinary men like us.

---

1. *Lodrö Thaye* and *Karma Ngakwang Yönten Gyatso*: two names for the first Jamgön Kongtrül Rinpoche. See also Appendix 1.
2. Eight good qualities: See "Questions and Answers," page 84.

You are the refuge called Padma,[3] endowed with blessings.
From the eight-petaled lotus dome[4] of my heart.
I supplicated you not to be separate even for an instant.
Though I did not have the good fortune of realization and
    liberation at once,[5]
I was blessed with just recognizing my own nature.

Therefore, concern for the eight worldly dharmas[6]
    diminished,
And I clearly saw the famous luminous dharmakaya[7]
By mixing my mind with the guru's.
I discovered nonthought in the midst of discursive thought,
And within nonconcept, wisdom dawned.
Now, with the joyous appreciation of a lineage son of the
    Takpo buddha,
I am inspired to speak out.

In the west, in Uddiyana, the secret treasure ground of the
    dakinis,
The great siddha Tilo[8]
Opened the treasure of the three gems.[9]
In the north, in the hermitage of Ravishing Beautiful
    Flowers,
The learned Mahapandita Naro[10]
Showed the mark of a siddha, indivisible prana[11] and mind.

3. *Padma* (Tib., *pema*, "lotus") refers to Jamgön Kongtrül Lodrö Thaye's teacher, Situ Pema Nyinje Wangpo.
4. Eight-petaled lotus dome: In the vajrayana, the relationship to the teacher is very important. One way of constantly upholding it is to visualize one's teacher seated on an eight-petaled lotus in one's heart.
5. *Realization and liberation at once*: momentary experience of the highest mahamudra realization.
6. See Glossary: *eight worldly dharmas*.
7. For *dharmakaya*, see Glossary: *kaya*.
8. *Tilo*: Tilopa. See Glossary.
9. *Three gems*: See Glossary.
10. *Naro*: Naropa. See Glossary.
11. *Prana*: wind of energy in the body. See Glossary: *prana, nadi, bindu*.

In the south, in the land of herbs, the valley of Trowo,
The translator,[12] *emanated from Hevajra,*
Established the source of the river of all siddhas.

In the west, in the Lachi snow range,
The supreme being, Shepa Dorje,
Attained the state of unity in one lifetime.

In the east, in heavenly Taklha Gampo,[13]
The honorable physician, the second victorious one,
Realized the samadhi of the tenth bhumi.

In the chakras of body, speech, and mind,
The host of the siddhas of the four great and eight lesser
      lineages[14]
Obtained the life-force of mahamudra
And could not help but attain enlightenment.
Skilled in magnetizing through bodhichitta,
They could not help but benefit beings.
Having obtained the profound wealth, the perfection of the
      two accumulations,[15]
They could not help but become prosperous [but realize
      sambhogakaya][16]
Fully understanding that knowing one liberates all,
They could not help but fulfill the great prophecy.[17]

Lineage sons of these wealthy fathers
Possess the great self-existing riches of this previous karma.
They are the children of snow lionesses and great garudas.

---

12. Refers to *Marpa* the Translator. See Glossary.
13. *Gampo*: Gampopa. See Glossary.
14. See Glossary: *Kagyü.*
15. See Glossary: *two accumulations.*
16. For *sambhogakaya*, see Glossary: *kaya.*
17. Realization of buddhahood, as was prophesied by the teacher.

By the power of their family bloodline, they are completely
    mature at once.
As followers of the lineage of Kagyü siddhas,
Their meditation is naturally born through the power of
    these blessings.

Bragging of their pain in many years of practice,
Proud of dwelling in indolence,
Boasting of having endured such pain,
Undermining others and haughty,
Keeping score with discursive thoughts of self and others
In counting up the realizations of the bhumis and the paths.[18]
These are the qualities of the ignorant meditators in this
    dark age.
We do not possess these, and though I do not have the title of
    a siddha,
Nevertheless, through the excellent oral instructions of the
    example lineage,[19]
I have seen the wisdom of ultimate mahamudra.

Ground mahamudra is the view, understanding things as
    they are.
Path mahamudra is the experience of meditation.
Fruition mahamudra is the realization of one's mind as
    buddha.
I am unworthy, but my guru is good.
Though born in the dark age, I am very fortunate.
Though I have little perseverance, the oral instructions are
    profound.

    The doha that is the subject of this book was sung by
Jamgön Kongtrül Lodrö Thaye, the first Jamgön Kongtrül
Rinpoche, upon realizing mahamudra.

---

18. See Glossary: *five paths.*
19. The mahamudra teachings of the Kagyü transmission.

The first part, consisting of praise to Vajradhara and the lineage holders Tilopa, Naropa, Marpa, Milarepa, and Gampopa, is not elucidated here in greater detail, since these teachings deal specifically with the central issue of the doha, which is mahamudra, and contain explanations about ground, path, and fruition mahamudra.

GROUND MAHAMUDRA

As for ground mahamudra:
There are both things as they are and the way of confusion.

What is the meaning of ground mahamudra? "Things as they are" refers to the ground, that is, the nature of all phenomena; "the way of confusion" refers to the state in which one finds oneself as long as one has not acknowledged the nature of phenomena (the Tibetan word for "confusion" actually means something that is not in accordance with nature). Thus there are these two states.

In connection with this, Gampopa's *Jewel Ornament of Liberation* states that the basic nature of all beings is in itself pure and free from confusion, but since one does not recognize one's basic nature one lives in a state of confusion. Still, confusion is not inherent in the nature of mind itself, which is pure and free from any confusion or stain. Confusion means simply that one has not yet understood one's true nature, whereas buddhahood is understanding one's true nature. Buddhahood does not involve acquiring something new, but rather recognizing something that was always there.

In brief, ground mahamudra is contained both in things as they are as well as in confusion; it is contained both in self-nature, which is free from confusion, and in the nonrecognition of this true nature. Confusion manifests in various illusory views, such as the belief that things are really existent or totally nonexistent.

It does not incline toward either samsara or nirvana, . . .

Although in terms of their ultimate nature samsara and nirvana are not separate, nevertheless one perceives them as opposites. Experiencing the confusion of samsara, one is also led to experience the fruition of samsara in the form of suffering. In one's experience, samsara appears as something painful and evil that one should free oneself from so as to overcome suffering, whereas nirvana, or freedom from confusion and pain, appears as a state that is higher than and opposed to samsara, a state of liberation that one should strive for.

In one's confusion, samsara and nirvana appear as separate entities, samsara as something bad and nirvana as something desirable and positive. Ultimately, however, this separation between samsara as confusion and nirvana as a state of liberation from confusion does not exist in the nature of self. By its own nature, samsara is emptiness; however, since one does not recognize its emptiness, it appears in the form of samsara or suffering. Nirvana is freedom from any type of confusion or suffering. This is its only difference with respect to samsara, since the nature of nirvana is also emptiness, as is the nature of samsara. Therefore, samsara and nirvana are ultimately inseparable, since the nature of both is emptiness. This is why the text says: "It does not incline toward either samsara or nirvana"—toward a samsara that would have to be abandoned or a nirvana that would have to be achieved.

*And is free from the extremes of exaggeration and
denigration.*

The basic nature of all phenomena is free from extremes
such as existence and nonexistence, because the ultimate
nature of reality is the inseparability of emptiness and luminosity. Misunderstanding this, the luminous aspect of
mind appears as the world of relative manifestations.

Not comprehending the true nature of appearances, one
develops definite preconceptions with regard to their essence. One either considers appearances to be permanent,
which leads to the extreme of eternalism or believing in the
lasting existence of things, or else one negates appearances
altogether, which leads to the extreme of nihilism or believing in their nonexistence. As long as one does not understand the essential unity of emptiness and luminosity, one
clings to these views and finds it impossible to get rid of the
illusion that things really do or do not exist, or that I exist
and the other exists, and so on.

Within the relative world phenomena arise only in interdependence. Since appearances come into being through
dependent origination, they are neither existent nor nonexistent. Thus neither of the two extremes of eternalism and
nihilism are accurate. However, because one does not understand the meaning of dependent origination one clings
to these extreme views.

This was described by the third Karmapa, Rangjung
Dorje, in his Mahamudra Supplication:

> All phenomena are projections of mind.
> Mind itself does not exist
> And is empty in its being.
> Although empty, it manifests everything without
>   obstruction.

Through precise examination
May we discover the fundamental root.

Where does the confusion with regard to the appearance
of things lie? Could it be that external objects are the source
of confusion, that confusion lies in phenomena? In fact,
confusion does not lie in objects that come into being, since
phenomena arise from the luminosity of mind. The unobstructed play of the mind is, in fact, the manifestation of
phenomena. If all appearances arise from mind, can one
then assume that confusion lies in the nature of mind itself?
Yet mind is by its very nature emptiness, therefore confusion cannot lie in the nature of mind.

The nature of mind is emptiness, yet things arise unobstructedly in all their diversity. This is the fundamental nature of both mind and ground mahamudra. Mind is by its
very nature empty, yet appearances arise from it without
obstruction. Out of the unobstructed emptiness of mind the
whole range of appearances can manifest without limit. On
a relative level, phenomena manifest through dependent
origination; this is inseparable from the emptiness of mind,
which is the ultimate level. Freedom from extremes is realizing that emptiness and dependent origination are one and
do not contradict each other. Confusion lies neither in the
appearance of things, nor in the fact that they are manifested
by mind, but in one's own misunderstanding of the emptiness and luminosity of mind.

Not produced by causes, not changed by conditions,
It is not spoiled by confusion
Nor exalted by realization.
It does not know either confusion or liberation.

The nature of mind, or ground mahamudra, is free from extremes. It is not produced by causes, unlike external phenomena that arise based on causal factors. Similarly, it is not changed by conditions, unlike external objects that change their appearance due to various influences. Neither of these apply to the nature of mind.

Neither confusion nor realization can influence the nature of mind. Although one will remain in a state of confusion as long as one does not recognize mind's nature, the basic nature of mind itself is neither confused nor contaminated by this. It always remains the same. Similarly, even if one manages to free oneself from confusion and fully recognizes the nature of mind, mind's nature itself is not improved; it acquires no new qualities that were not there previously. Accordingly, since the nature of mind itself is never confused by confusion, there is also no liberation from confusion as far as the nature of mind is concerned.

Since no essence exists anywhere,
Its expression is completely unobstructed and manifests
    everything.
Pervading all of samsara and nirvana like space, . . .

The nature of mind does not depend on causes and conditions, nor does it consist of substances, as external objects do. This is why the expression of the mind is unobstructed and everything can manifest. Yet, although the nature of mind consists of nothing, it is not nothingness, and allows both samsara and nirvana to arise. It is the basis for everything.

According to the Mahamudra Supplication by Rangjung Dorje:

[Mind] is not existent
Since even the Buddhas do not see it,
Nor is it nonexistent
Since it is the basis for all,
Both samsara and nirvana.

The basic nature of mind is complete, both in one's present state of confusion or samsara, and in the state of liberation from confusion. To liberate oneself from confusion it is necessary to remove the obscurations that veil the nature of mind. One experiences the state of confusion or samsara only because one does not recognize the nature of mind; if one recognizes it, that is liberation from confusion. Liberation is not something new to be acquired externally but resides within mind itself. Mind is the basis for both samsara and nirvana, for both confusion and liberation.

It is the ground of all confusion and liberation,
With its self-luminous consciousness
And its alaya-vijñana.
As for the cognitive aspect of this neutral state,
Its essence is empty and its nature is luminous.
These two are inseparable and are the quintessence of
    insight.

At present, because of one's confusion, one clings to concepts and is therefore unable to experience one's inherent self-knowing insight, the self-luminosity of mind from which everything arises. One experiences instead the so-called alaya-vijñana, that aspect of one's mind that underlies all the different types of consciousness one has at present. In the alaya-vijñana are stored all the positive, negative, or neutral impressions. When activated, it projects these impressions, yet by its very nature the alaya-vijñana is nothing other than self-knowing insight.

Because of its luminous quality, mind itself is not hidden; it can know itself and display all the manifold buddha qualities and wisdoms. Emptiness and luminosity of mind are inseparable and in fact constitute mind, which is the unity of space or emptiness and wisdom or insight. The expression "quintessence of insight" refers precisely to this unity of emptiness and luminosity.

It is space, ungraspable as a thing.
It is a spotless precious clear crystal.
It is the glow of the lamp of self-luminous mind.
It is inexpressible, the experience of a mute.
It is unobscured, transparent wisdom,
The luminous dharmakaya, sugatagarbha,
Primordially pure and spontaneous.
It cannot be shown through analogy by anyone,
And it cannot be expressed in words.
It is the dharmadhatu, which overwhelms mind's inspection.

Although one cannot point to mind and say it is this or that, mind pervades all of samsara and nirvana. Buddha-nature, the nature of mind, is undefiled by obscurations, like a completely pure and clear crystal, transparent and shining. Like the glow of a lamp which lights up its surroundings, insight and self-luminosity of mind are in themselves enlightenment, without the need to add anything. They cannot be expressed in words, and even direct experience of them defies description, like a deaf-mute who cannot put his experience into words.

The nature of mind is unobscured perfect wisdom. It includes all the previously described qualities and is the dharmakaya. Luminous dharmakaya itself is identical with sugatagarbha or buddha-nature. Buddha-nature is both primordially pure, since it has never been defiled by obscurations, and spontaneous, since all the sixty-four qualities of a buddha are always complete and naturally present within it, without the need to attain or acquire them.

Buddha-nature, however, cannot be described with examples or concepts. Buddha himself said that everything related to prajñaparamita, the highest form of knowledge, can be neither grasped with thoughts, described in words, nor explained with concepts, since it transcends conceptual mind.

Buddha-nature cannot be understood by thinking, speculation, or intellectual approaches. It is impossible to attain actual understanding of the true nature of mind through examples, concepts, thoughts, or personal ideas. Other things can be understood in this manner, but the dharmadhatu "overwhelms" mind since it is beyond mind. Insight into buddha-nature can only arise through inner experience in meditation.

Established in this to begin with,
One should cut all doubts.

How does one go about acquiring insight into buddhanature or dharmadhatu, which are beyond words, concepts, or personal ideas? First, one must receive teachings in order to establish oneself in the proper view. Phenomena do not really exist. While on a relative plane all things arise in mutual interdependence, ultimately they are nonexistent, even though in one's confusion one takes them to be real. These two levels of reality, that is, the relative and the ultimate, are inseparable; they are not in opposition, but form a whole.

Once one has understood the various aspects of the
proper view and is aware of the unity of relative truth and
ultimate truth, then one does not fall into the extreme views
of existence and nonexistence and can practice meditation
based on this view.

When one practices meditation with the view,
It is like a garuda fathoming space.
There is no fear and no doubt.
The one who meditates without the view
Is like a blind man wandering the plains.
There is no reference point for where the true path is.
The one who does not meditate, but merely holds the view,
Is like a rich man tethered by stinginess.
He is unable to bring appropriate fruition to himself and
*   others.*
Joining the view and meditation is the holy tradition.

Buddha taught on very different levels, in accordance
with the intelligence of his students. There are teachings
that convey the actual meaning directly, while others require
interpretation, or rather, further elucidation. One must
place the different explanations on relative and ultimate
truth in this last category. If one has not understood the
proper view, or has understood it only vaguely, one will not
know which teachings may be grasped directly and which
require further elucidation. Not recognizing the unity of the
two truths, one will feel that these two modes of explanation
are contradictory and will run the risk of getting confused
for want of adequate theoretical understanding. For instance, seeing that in one place the teachings state that
things exist and in another place that things do not exist,
one will only see contradiction in this.

In his teachings, Buddha Shakyamuni always presented both levels of reality. Although on different occasions he may have emphasized relative or ultimate truth, this was done on the assumption that his students understood the unity of these two truths. If this understanding is lacking, everything becomes difficult and complicated, because one does not include the ultimate level in contemplating relative reality of phenomena, and one forgets about the relative level in referring to ultimate truth. If, however, one understands the unity of these two levels of reality, then difficulties will not arise. A proper understanding of the unity of relative and ultimate truth is of great importance, especially for vajrayana practitioners of the mahamudra.

Madhyamaka philosophy deals with an understanding of emptiness, with the fact that all phenomena are free of any extreme form of existence. Although the different madhyamaka schools, for instance the rangtong and the shentong schools, explain emptiness differently, their statements do not contradict each other. They are not teaching different things; rather, they are emphasizing different aspects in their explanation of emptiness. Thus, when the rangtong madhyamaka school stresses the fact that all phenomena are by their very nature empty, the emphasis is on the emptiness aspect itself. Similarly, when the shentong madhyamaka school states that mind contains buddha-nature and that this buddha-nature must be purified of the veils that obscure it, the emphasis is on the luminosity aspect. When one understands these two types of explanation, one realizes that emptiness and luminosity are inseparable. It is precisely this understanding that is imperative for mahamudra meditation.

Only by achieving certainty with regard to the right view can one apply the different meditation techniques properly and practice them free from obstacles. This is why it is said that a person who has achieved certainty in the view and practices meditation with a proper outlook is like a garuda—such a person deals with whatever experiences arise in meditation without being disturbed by them. On the other hand, if one attempts to meditate without having first achieved an accurate understanding, one will stumble over these uncertainties. One will not be sure about the way, never really knowing whether one is making a mistake or not. Unable to get one's bearings, one will be like a blind person wandering the plains.

Still, although the proper view is extremely important, it is not sufficient by itself since only through meditation does inner experience arise. To merely hold the view and not meditate brings no benefit either to oneself or others; one is like a rich person tethered by stinginess. Thus, according to the holy tradition, the proper view must be combined with insight arising from meditation.

As for the ignorant aspect of this neutral state,
One does not know one's nature because of the five causes.

Although luminosity or buddha-nature, which is the basic nature of mind, is free from confusion, one does not recognize it and thus finds oneself in a state of confusion. Why does one not recognize it? Because of five factors. First of all, because one does not understand that buddha-nature is inherent in the mind of all beings. Buddha-nature is the same in all beings; it pervades all beings equally, with no quantitative or qualitative differences. Not recognizing this is the first cause of ignorance.

The second cause lies in having a dualistic view of samsara and nirvana as two distinct states. One incorrectly considers buddhahood as something separate and therefore thinks that one has to look for it outside.

Third, one holds on to the concept that buddhahood is far away, and that the path is long and arduous, even though it is only a matter of recognizing the nature of mind and this can be done in an instant. One does not need a long path to achieve this. A good illustration is provided by the eyelashes: In spite of the fact that the eyelashes are right against the eyes, one does not see them. Similarly, buddha-nature is the true nature of mind, yet one is not aware of this. Although buddha-nature is simply awareness of the nature of mind, constant distraction prevents one from realizing this.

The fourth cause is not realizing that the world of experiences only arises on the basis of impressions stored away in mind, which lead one to establish a distinction between subject and object. Because of the impressions stored in the alaya-vijñana, one's experiences are perceived as objects, whereas the experiencer himself is perceived as a subject. However, one does not understand that this dichotomy arises exclusively on the basis of habitual patterns stored in one's mind. One firmly believes in the world of experiences, and by reacting to it performs more positive and negative actions which in turn create more habitual patterns.

The fifth cause is not understanding that mind, which is itself buddha-nature, already contains all the buddha qualities. The buddha qualities of the dharmakaya and the form kayas are inherent in one's mental continuum. However, one believes that it is necessary first of all to cleanse oneself of defects and then to develop good qualities in order to achieve buddhahood. These five factors prevent one from realizing the nature of mind or buddha-nature, and lead one into confusion, the wheel of existence.

In the ocean of coemergent ignorance,
The waves of ego-fixation's confusion roll.
Cognition becomes a self, and projections become objects,
And so the habitual patterns of grasping and fixation solidify.
Thus, karma accumulates and then fully ripens.
The rim of the waterwheel of samsara turns,
But even while it turns, its essence is unstained.
Even while it appears, it is empty of reality.

Although the nature of mind, the basis, is completely pure, one does not recognize this luminosity. Failing to recognize one's own mind is what is known as ignorance. Out of ignorance arises the fixation to a self. The nature of mind, which is cognition, or awareness of the fact that one is aware, is falsely experienced as a self with which one then identifies; this is grasping. Simultaneously, mind's luminosity, its ability to project, is experienced as something separate from this identity, as an external object; this is fixation. This dualistic view shapes one's actions, and thus karma is accumulated in many ways. The accumulated impressions and the accumulated karma ripen; the ongoing process of karma ripening is the wheel of samsara, through which one circles constantly. The image of the waterwheel of samsara turning constantly refers to this process. A more precise way of describing this vicious circle is as follows.

The first aspect is the alaya-vijñana, which is the basis for the entire process. Since mind does not understand its own true nature, the stirrings of the mind lead to the creation of habitual patterns. These in turn lead to the arising of disturbing emotions and concepts, which create further habitual patterns in the alaya-vijñana. Another aspect of mind, known as "mental force," stores impressions in the alaya-vijñana. There is a third aspect, called "cloudy mind," that rests on the alaya-vijñana; this aspect experiences confusion and the concepts of "me" and "I am." It is these three aspects—the alaya-vijñana in which impressions are stored, the cloudy mind with its concept of a self, and the mental force that plants tendencies in the mind, creates concepts, and develops habitual patterns—that together produce the experience of samsara.

Let us take the example of a shape being perceived through visual consciousness; the perception is immediately followed by a value judgment, with the shape being evaluated as either good, bad, or neutral. Although visual consciousness is perfectly capable of perceiving the external forms by themselves, judgments such as "this is a shape . . . it is good" are apprehended at the level of mind consciousness. When mind consciousness evaluates a perception, this value judgment gives rise to a mental impression which the mental force stores in the alaya-vijñana in the form of tendencies. These reinforce previous impressions already stored in the alaya-vijñana and further solidify ego-fixation or cloudy mind.

To summarize, one could say that the basis for confusion resides in mental force and the alaya-vijñana. The impressions that the mental force deposits in the alaya-vijñana eventually activate the latter. Because of this, one establishes a distinction between external sense objects, the various types of internal sense-consciousness, and mind consciousness, which further solidifies the concepts related to dualistic fixation.

One can also explain the entire process in terms of the skandhas. The skandha of consciousness activates the impressions stored in the alaya-vijñana, which causes one to experience the six types of consciousness. The skandha of feeling and discrimination involves clinging to the objects of the senses so that by perceiving them various feelings of pleasure, aversion, and indifference arise. The skandha of perception-impulse involves reacting to feelings, grasping at things that are pleasant, and rejecting those that are unpleasant, and so on. As the fixation becomes stronger and stronger, the skandha of form finally arises, which creates a distinction between self and other.

This external other is in turn perceived by the six types of consciousness, thus creating a loop—the vicious circle of samsara. However, the only reason that the wheel of samsara continues to turn is because impressions that have accumulated in mind are once again projected outward when the alaya-vijñana is activated by mental force. The confusion lies in believing that phenomena that arise on a relative plane are real, rather than mere appearances based on the unobstructed manifestation of mind. However, on an ultimate plane—that of the true nature of all appearances—there can be no confusion. The nature of appearances is empty, and these are by their very nature not truly existent; although they manifest as appearances, they are empty of nature. One might think that phenomena are empty only in non-manifestation and not in manifestation, but this is not the case. When phenomena manifest, they are empty in their very essence, and because they are empty they can manifest unobstructedly in all their diversity.

Mere appearance is the vividness of the trikaya.

Because the nature of things is empty, things can manifest in all their luminosity and umimpededness; therefore, the three kayas are spontaneously and naturally present in all relative phenomena. The nature of phenomena is emptiness, their attribute is luminosity, and their manifestation is unobstructedness.

All appearances are a manifestation of mind. However, not understanding the nature of mind, which is emptiness, one experiences the confused aspect of mind, or alaya-vijñana. In other words, since one does not recognize the attribute of mind, which is luminosity, one experiences its confused aspect, cloudy mind. And since one does not understand the manifestation of mind, which is complete unobstructedness, one experiences its confused aspect, which are the different types of sense consciousnesses. Thus, the difference is exclusively a matter of recognizing versus not recognizing. By not recognizing one experiences the alaya-vijñana, cloudy mind, and the sense consciousnesses; however, these are actually the trikaya, whose nature is empty, whose attribute is luminosity, and whose manifestation is unobstructedness. This is why the three kayas are spontaneously present in everything.

Unborn is the nature of birth;
That unborn is unceasing.
On the threshold of nonduality, there is nowhere to dwell.

To ordinary perception, phenomena appear to come into being. However, this coming into being is only appearance; it is merely manifestation on a relative level, based on particular causes and conditions. From an ultimate viewpoint, that is, one in accordance with the true nature of things, phenomena do not come into being; nevertheless, their manifestation and continuity are unobstructed, since they manifest on a relative plane continuously and in many forms. On the threshold of nonduality—between the relative arising of phenomena and the fact that they are ultimately unborn—there is no dwelling. The actual nature of mind, which is luminosity, is free from birth, dwelling, and cessation.

From this mind, difficult to express,
Various magical displays of samsara and nirvana arise.
Recognizing these as self-liberated is the supreme view.
When this is realized, everything is suchness.
When there are no obstructions or attainments, this is the
    innate nature.
When conceptual mind is transcended, this is the ultimate.

What is free from birth, dwelling, and cessation? It is the nature of mind. However, as long as one does not recognize the nature of mind, one experiences samsara; if one does recognize it, one experiences nirvana. In other words, the way phenomena manifest depends on awareness. Nirvana is not attained by overcoming samsara or putting an end to disturbing emotions in order to develop something else. On the contrary, one should look at the actual nature of the disturbing emotion and thus "self-liberate" it and recognize its true nature. By holding to this supreme view, one can understand reality, the suchness of all phenomena. If one achieves this realization and fully recognizes the basic nature of all phenomena, without struggling to give up samsara or attain nirvana, then everything becomes ultimate reality. Conceptual mind dissolves, along with its value judgments as to what is good and bad, and one attains the goal, which is the realization of the ultimate view.

In brief, the nature of all phenomena is devoid of true existence. By their very nature, phenomena are the three kayas. Free from birth, they are the dharmakaya; their unobstructed manifestation is the sambhogakaya; and their manifold arising is the nirmanakaya. The three kayas are not separate from each other; together, they are the nature of all phenomena. This is what the expression "innate nature" refers to. When there are no obstructions or attainments — when one realizes that the nature of all phenomena is the trikaya — one can rest in that basic, spontaneous nature. This is the ultimate view, ground mahamudra.

Summary of Ground Mahamudra

The true basic nature is buddha-nature; it is free from extremes such as eternalism and nihilism. It is already pure, by nature unimpeded and is not liberated by realization. It is not an object, not a thing, it is devoid of characteristics, and there is nothing that this nature does not pervade. The entire external world — all phenomena, all experiences — is pervaded by this true nature, in the same way as space is all-pervading. While on a relative plane samsara and nirvana appear to be separate from each other, ultimately, they are nondual in suchness. This is the true nature of mind, which is buddha-nature, ultimate truth, ultimate bodhichitta. These are only concepts related to ground mahamudra, the basic nature of all phenomena.

This ends the section of the song referring to ground mahamudra, or basic nature and the proper viewpoint with regard to it.

PATH MAHAMUDRA

As for path mahamudra:

Path mahamudra is the practice of the view of mahamudra, the experience of this view through meditation. According to the Kagyü school, one can establish a basic distinction between two types of mahamudra: sutra mahamudra and tantra mahamudra.

Sutra mahamudra deals first and foremost with the realization of emptiness, it is realizing that phenomena are devoid of true existence. This view frees one from all illusions with regard to suchness, so that one can rest in the nature of mind, free from ideas and preconceptions. This is sutra mahamudra: freedom from illusions, from the fabrications of mind.

Tantra mahamudra, on the other hand, is an integral part of the vajrayana. In each successive vajrayana practice, the practitioner must first receive an empowerment for the respective yidam. The empowerment consists of four parts, one of which is the introduction to tantra mahamudra, the wisdom of the union of great bliss and emptiness. Whether one is practicing sutra or tantra mahamudra, meditation with form or formless meditation, mahamudra involves dwelling in the nature of mind, the state of luminosity.

Path mahamudra is the practice, the activity that one carries out on the path. The incomparable Takpo Kagyü lineage brings together two different lines of transmission, since Gampopa united the Kadampa-school teachings of Atisa with those of the mahamudra lineage. The path includes both of these transmissions.

The Premilinaries (Ngöndro)
In order to develop mahamudra meditation properly, one should begin by following the teachings of the Kadampa school and reminding oneself of the four thoughts that turn the mind away from samsara. These are what are known as the four ordinary preliminaries. They are followed by the four special preliminaries. The first of these latter four consists of two aspects: taking refuge in the Three Gems and

the Three Roots, and developing bodhichitta, the desire to lead all beings to buddhahood. These two aspects together bring about the accumulation of merit. The second practice, the meditation on Vajrasattva and the recitation of the hundred-syllable mantra, purifies obscurations. The third practice, the mandala offering, is used for both types of accumulations—the accumulation of merit, which is based on reference points, and the accumulation of wisdom, which is nonreferential. Finally, the practice of guruyoga gives one the blessings of the guru's body, speech, and mind and unites one with one's teacher.

Thus, the path of mahamudra begins with the sequential practice of the four ordinary and the four special preliminaries. Only then does one reach the point at which one can truly practice path mahamudra. The path of mahamudra involves not only acquiring a certain amount of knowledge and working on the theoretical content of the teachings, but also practicing meditation and acquiring insight into one's mind. To this end it is absolutely essential to accumulate merit through the preliminary practices and to purify oneself from obscurations. This is why all the teachers of the Kagyü lineage have always stressed the importance of ngöndro. Thanks to these preparatory practices, one's mind can "be one with the dharma" and one's dharma practice can "progress along the path," as is said in the *Four Dharmas of Gampopa.*

Mind and the phenomenal world are mahamudra.
Coemergent mind is dharmakaya.
Coemergent appearance is the light of dharmakaya.

The introduction to path mahamudra is the realization that one's own mind is dharmakaya; that the phenomenal world—external appearances—is a manifestation of mind, that is, the light of dharmakaya; and that one's own mind and the phenomenal world are not different from each other.

As is said in one of the tantras: "Dharmakaya is inherent in mind; the light of dharmakaya is inherent in phenomena. The inherent nature of mind and phenomena is inseparable." "Dharmakaya is inherent in mind" refers to mind's emptiness, the fact that it is devoid of true nature, which is dharmakaya. "The light of dharmakaya is inherent in phenomena" refers to the unobstructed quality of mind, whose manifestation is the entire display of phenomena. Phenomena are also the natural expression and manifestation of dharmakaya. "The inherent nature of mind and phenomena is inseparable" refers to the fact that mind and the manifestation of its unobstruced quality, or phenomena, are not separate from each other, but form a unity. This is the threefold introduction to path mahamudra.

The meditation practice that is based on this realization is first and foremost the meditation called shamatha or "remaining in calmness," which enables one to become aware of the essential nature of mind. It is mind that both experiences all external phenomena—all one's joys and problems, samsara and nirvana—and also produces the totality of samsara and nirvana.

This is why in meditation one first looks at the nature of mind. Is mind a mere nothingness? This is impossible, since it is mind, after all, that experiences and produces everything. Does mind exist? If it did, it would have had to come into existence at a given point in time and space. Besides, once something is born it must inevitably pass away after having endured for a certain length of time. However, if one examines the nature of mind one is unable to find these

three phases of arising, dwelling, and cessation because
mind is free from them. This freedom from arising, dwelling, and cessation is the dharmakaya, the lack of true existence of mind. Thus, one realizes that mind is not truly existent. This is insight into the inherent dharmakaya-nature
of mind.

But if mind is not truly existent, where does the world of
external appearances arise from? Phenomena are the inherent manifestation of mind and appear from mind's luminosity and its unobstructed quality. The manifold appearances
are only an expression of mind; they are nothing other than
mind. One could compare this with the sun and sunshine:
sunshine—phenomena—are not different from the sun itself—mind—even though they may seem to be. In the same
way, the entire phenomenal world is a manifestation of
mind, inseparable from mind itself; although phenomena
obviously do exist on a relative plane, they are devoid of
ultimate existence. They are a manifestation of mind, the
light of dharmakaya.

When the blessings of the glorious guru
And one's karma come together,
One realizes one's nature like meeting an old friend.

How does one attain the realization of the nature of
mind? This realization cannot be forced. The Supplication
to the Takpo Kagyüs says that "devotion is the head of meditation." In order to recognize mind, the inspiration and
blessings of one's teacher are necessary, and one can only
receive these by having devotion for and trust in the teacher.
This is the "head of meditation." Without trust in and devotion for one's teacher, one cannot receive the teacher's
blessings and the entire lineage of transmission, and without

this inspiration one cannot totally recognize the nature of one's mind. By not recognizing it one will fail to understand that the nature of mind is dharmakaya and that all appearances are a manifestation of mind, the light of dharmakaya. Only by developing devotion for one's teacher can one receive blessings in one's mind, allowing previously accumulated positive karma to ripen. This is the basis that enables one to recognize directly one's own mind and the nature of phenomena, like meeting an old friend.

In this section of the song, Jamgön Kongtrül Lodrö Thaye explains how the nature of mind is recognized and mentions the factors on which this realization depends. These factors are extremely personal. One factor is the type of connection one has established with the teacher who introduces one to mahamudra and how long, that is, for how many kalpas, this connection has existed. Another factor is the trust in and devotion for the teacher. Only if the proper conditions are met will one recognize mind when the teacher points out its nature. In fact, one could meet many gurus, receive instructions from them on the nature of mind, and practice numerous meditations and still not experience the nature of mind. This is actually the case for a large number of practitioners.

Thus, the experience of meditation depends not only on the meditation itself but also on the depth of trust and devotion one has developed for one's teacher and on the existence of a karmic connection with that teacher from a previous lifetime. For this reason, one's root guru is of enormous importance, since only through the guru's instructions can one achieve insight into the nature of mind.

There is no point in much talk,
But the beginner needs various things.

If the aforementioned factors are lacking—if one does not have the trust and devotion that enable one to receive the teacher's blessings or if one does not have a karmic connection with the teacher—all the instructions about the nature of mind will be to no avail, since they will not enable one to recognize mind's nature. This does not mean, however, that one should simply wait without receiving instructions until some unspecified time in the future when the proper connection to a teacher may perhaps finally occur. This is not what is meant at all.

On the contrary, for the beginner it is extremely important to start by acquiring the proper view with regard to the nature of things. This will happen if one first receives teachings and acquires the prajña of hearing, then examines what one has learnt with the prajña of contemplation and overcomes all extreme views. It is equally important to practice the preliminaries in order to purify obscurations and accumulate merit. However, the phrase "the beginner needs various things" refers most particularly to inner renunciation of samsara, which is the indispensable foundation for developing genuine meditation. This is why the Supplication to the Takpo Kagyüs says that "revulsion is the foot of meditation," since without inwardly turning away from samsara there will be no basis for meditation.

A common misunderstanding is that renouncing samsara means giving up everything. What renunciation really means is developing the certainty that the conditioned world of samsara is devoid of true value. It means understanding that everything that seems pleasurable is actually suffering, that everything is transitory, in a constant state of change. Only when one truly feels that samsara is devoid of true value can one turn toward the dharma completely. Without this insight one will be unable to do so; one will lack the basis for true meditative experience, that does not set in as long as the mind is sidetracked by externals. The only way to overcome distractions is to renounce samsara.

One should abandon either welcoming or sending off
thoughts of past and future.

Mahamudra concerns ordinary awareness, the present moment of awareness; it involves resting in and experiencing that moment of nowness. One should neither reflect on the past nor make plans for the future, but let the mind experience the current moment of awareness. One should let it experience the thought that is naturally and spontaneously present, without expecting or looking for anything, and without avoiding or repressing anything—simply resting the mind in that moment of experience. There is no form of mahamudra meditation that does not involve experiencing the freshness of the present moment of awareness or thought. It is not a matter of attaining something different and better. When one rests in that moment of nowness, one's awareness is "ordinary awareness," it is the normal moment of awareness in which mind is aware of itself, in which mind simply rests in itself as it happens to be at that moment.

The instantaneous mind of nowness
Is the unfabricated innate nature.

In general, everybody strives to reinforce positive thoughts and reduce negative thoughts. This is not the point of this type of meditation. Nothing new is created, nothing is changed, nothing is judged. Without influencing the moment of nowness one rests in its original nature. Even though this does not involve an object of meditation, the mind does not stray but remains undistracted in the experience of the natural and ordinary awareness of the moment.

In meditation, there should be no trace of deliberateness.
One should not stray for an instant in confusion.
Nonwandering, nonmeditation, nonfabrication are the
point.
With freshness, looseness, and clarity,
In the space of the three gates of liberation,
One is mindful, establishing proper watchfulness.
Always keeping the mind balanced between tight and
relaxed,
One pacifies the accumulation of subtle, tangible, and gross
thoughts.
Rest in the state of natural, unfabricated mind.

Whenever a thought arises, whether positive or negative, one should avoid deliberately concerning oneself with it, and let the mind rest spontaneously in the nature of the thought; without being sidetracked by the thought one should rest in the mind of nowness. Nonwandering means maintaining a fresh and full awareness of the moment of nowness without straying, resting in the freshness of the instantaneous mind of nowness without altering it. Nonmeditation means that resting does not involve meditating on an object, but simply relaxing in the nature of mind. Nonfabrication means that whatever arises in the mind, for instance thoughts and feelings, should not be judged as being good or bad. One should not strive to push thoughts away in order to make space for something else, but just rest in the moment of awareness. This is the meaning of nonwandering, nonmeditation, and nonfabrication, which are known as the "three gates of liberation."

If one practices in this manner, then all hopes, fears, views, and concepts related to the three times—past, present, and future—dissolve and one enters through the three gates of liberation, having properly realized ground, path, and fruition. With regard to the ground, one realizes that there is no arising; with regard to the path, one sees that it possesses no distinctive features; and with regard to the fruition, one is free from the desire to achieve anything.

Nonwandering is extremely important. This is why the Supplication to the Takpo Kagyüs states that "awareness is the body of meditation." To this end, two elements are necessary in meditation. The first is composure or mindfulness in order to achieve one-pointedness of mind, and the second, watchfulness to prevent mind from straying once again into distraction. It is essential to maintain both composure and watchfulness so that mind can experience its original nature. Without them, one is subject to habitual patterns; as soon as one thinks of something mind starts to wander. Only through composure and watchfulness can one achieve nonwandering and rest in the nature of mind.

The song also says that one should keep the mind balanced between being tight and relaxed. It often happens in meditation that one either becomes sleepy and dull or else one's mind is very distracted. The point is to find a middle path. This means neither tensing up in one's efforts to achieve composure, since this leads to distractions, nor being too relaxed, since one's mind will become sluggish. Such a balance is essential in order to rest in the nature of mind, since only in this way can one pacify the three types of thoughts: subtle, tangible, and gross.

··· *Commentary* ···

The four levels of experiences arise in succession,
And the sun of luminosity continually dawns.
The root of mahamudra meditation is established.

If one practices meditation with composure and watchfulness, one's mind will spontanteously rest in its own nature and the various stages of experience on the path will arise progressively one after another. Having established the root of mahamudra meditation, then gradually the four stages of experience on the path—one-pointedness, freedom from illusion, one-taste, and nonmeditation—will come forth, and the sun of luminosity of mahamudra will shine continually.

Without it, one's talk of higher realization
Is like building a house without a foundation.

If one is unable to practice meditation with composure and watchfulness yet claims to practice mahamudra meditation and to have realized the unity of samsara and nirvana, one is just uttering empty words because one's meditation lacks a proper foundation. Only on the basis of composure and watchfulness will the mind come to rest and the gross or subtle thoughts be pacified. In this state of resting, mind can remain in its innate spontaneous nature and give rise to the various stages of experience. This is why shamatha meditation, "remaining in calmness," is so important: if one is unable to let the mind come to rest through composure and watchfulness, then vipashyana, "clear seeing," will never arise.

However, excessive desire for this is the work of Mara.
Those who persevere but have little learning

Are deceived by superficial virtues
And lead themselves and others along the way to the lower
realms.
Even the good experiences of bliss, luminosity, and
nonthought
Are the cause of samsara if one fixates on them.

Various experiences arise in meditation; without the basis of composure and watchfulness, one will rapidly fixate on them. Although one may have the impression that one has realized emptiness or achieved profound insight into something or other, fixation will have turned the experience into an obstacle for development, preventing further experiences from arising. Fixation on mere experiences creates sidetracks, and this is why it is called the work of Mara.

Some people do not have enough theoretical knowledge about the path and the proper view and thus practice without an adequate foundation; for all their diligence, they end up wandering off the path and misleading themselves. They mistake illusory experiences for actual experiences and continue their practice although they have taken a wrong turn. Far from leading them to liberation, their practice will lead them to the lower realms. Practicing mahamudra without the proper view can cause one to misunderstand one's experiences and harm oneself. If in addition one speaks about one's experiences to others, believing in the apparent depth of one's own realization and wanting to show others the way and impart one's knowledge to them, then one is also harming others.

Therefore, mahamudra meditation should not be practiced haphazardly, just sitting in the meditation posture without having the certainty of the proper view. It is very important first to acquire the proper view on the true nature of mind in order to practice meditation on this foundation. Otherwise, one not only strays off the path of liberation, but also leads oneself and others toward the lower realms. If one practices the path properly, the experiences of bliss, luminosity, and nonthought arise; yet if one clings to these experiences, they become a further cause for conditioned existence.

When you intensify devotion in your heart,
Rock meets bone in insight,
And the ultimate lineage blessing is received.

Through total devotion which penetrates one's heart, one's mind is filled with the blessings of the guru and the previous teachers of the Kagyü lineage. When one experiences such devotion and inspiration, "rock meets bone." This means that total devotion makes the guru's blessings so intense that, just as rock destroys bone, the blessings prevent any possible wrong turns. Thus one should cultivate deep devotion in order to experience the freshness of the present moment.

Not straying into the four strayings,
Not falling into the three misunderstandings,
Transcending the four joys, free from the three
    conditions, . . .

After practicing for a certain time, experiences of emptiness arise. It is possible to adopt wrong views with regard to these experiences. This is what the song calls "the four strayings": straying into the ground of emptiness, the path of emptiness, the antidote of emptiness, or the idea of emptiness.

Straying into the ground of emptiness means fixating on the essence of emptiness, emptiness as such. Having achieved a slight understanding of emptiness, one develops a nihilistic point of view, thinking that phenomena are only empty and that nothing exists. Straying into the path of emptiness means fixating on the experience of emptiness. Having experienced that all phenomena are empty, one thinks one has understood emptiness and that one no longer needs to accumulate merit, purify obscurations, perform positive actions, and avoid negative ones, and so on. Through ones' meditation one has achieved a slight insight into emptiness and mistakes it for a great realization. Straying into the antidote of emptiness means imagining, incorrectly, that by meditating on emptiness one will not attain any ultimate results. Not realizing the unity of luminosity and emptiness, one thinks that the fruition is not in the mind, in emptiness itself, but somewhere else. Failing to understand that means and wisdom are inseparable, one perceives emptiness and disturbing emotions as two separate things and attempts to use emptiness as an antidote against disturbing emotions. Straying into the idea of emptiness means simply imagining that all external phenomena are empty, without really having understood the emptiness of phenomena at all. These four types of straying occur especially in vipashyana meditation, since in this form of meditation one is preparing oneself to realize emptiness.

It is equally important to avoid falling into "the three misunderstandings." These refer mostly to shamatha meditation, since they involve fixating on experiences that occur when mind remains in calmness—the experiences of bliss, luminosity, and nonthought. Clinging to the experience of bliss leads to rebirth in the realm of the senses; clinging to the experience of luminosity leads to rebirth in the form realm; and clinging to the experience of nonthought leads to rebirth in the formless realm. Thus, fixation on the various meditative experiences is a cause for samsara.

"The four joys one should transcend" are joy, great joy, extraordinary joy, and inherent joy. These are the four joys that are sometimes described in empowerments as the "wisdom of example." Through these joys one recognizes one's own wisdom, that is, the state in which the understanding of emptiness, bliss, and nonthought are united. It is hardly possible to describe the four joys, since they refer to a siddha's experience, that can only gradually be achieved through one's own practice.

"The three conditions that one should be free from" are the same experiences that arise in shamatha meditation: bliss, luminosity, and nonthought. One should consider them as mere experiences and go beyond them.

Realizing through the three stages of birth,
Untouched by the mind of the three great ones, ...

"Realizing through the three stages of birth" refers to the speed with which practitioners develop on their way to buddhahood, in accordance with their capabilities. A distinction can be made between practitioners with low, middle, and high capabilities. Those with low capabilities follow the path step by step until they finally attain enlightenment. Those with middle capabilities skip over several stages of development; for instance, they can simultaneously realize the first two bhumis of the bodhisattva path, and then the third and fourth together, and thus attain enlightenment sooner. Those with the highest capabilities can attain enlightenment in one moment, that is, they simultaneously achieve realization and liberation.

"Untouched by the mind of the three great ones" means that ultimate nature—insight into one's original mind—occurs neither in the realm of understanding through hearing, nor in the real of experiencing through contemplation, nor in the realm of meditation. The original nature of mind is beyond these three.

This is the self-existing nature, undefiled by experience.
Like the center of a cloudless sky,
The self-luminous mind is impossible to express.
It is wisdom of nonthought beyond analogy,
Naked ordinary mind.

Direct experience of the self-existing, primordial, undefiled nature of mind is like a cloudless sky, in which luminosity—the blueness of the sky—exists by itself. Mind is complete in its self-awareness and self-luminosity, nothing else is necessary. This experience is inexpressible in words, and transcends analogies and descriptions. The wisdom of nonthought is the natural and fresh experience of ordinary mind.

Not keeping to dogmatism or arrogance,
It is clearly seen as dharmakaya.

"Not keeping to dogmatism" means that it is impossible to express this state in words. "Not keeping to arrogance" means that notions about the nature of mind are irrelevant. Free from the tendency to conceptualize experience in either words or thoughts, one rests in ordinary mind and experiences its nature as luminous dharmakaya.

The appearance of the six sense objects, like the moon in
*   water,*
Shines in the state of wisdom.
Whatever arises is the unfabricated innate state.
Whatever appears is the nature of mahamudra.
The phenomenal world is dharmakaya great bliss.

By its very nature, ordinary mind, that is, awareness of
the present moment, is the dharmakaya. Through this experience one realizes that everything that the six senses
come into contact with—appearance, sound, smell, and so
forth—is like the reflection of the moon in water; although
the moon can be seen quite distinctly it is not really present.
Having acknowledged this, one is no longer subject to the
confusion of thinking that things really do exist and one
experiences all that arises in the light of this wisdom.

One should not consider anything that arises in the mind,
such as thoughts, as being either positive or negative, and
one should avoid attaching hope or fear to it. Free from
rejecting or hoping, one should rest spontaneously in one's
primordial nature. Thus the entire world of appearances is
recognized as luminosity, the expression of dharmakaya,
and mind itself is seen as dharmakaya. Everything, whether
internal or external, is seen to be of the nature of mahamudra. However, in order to recognize this, shamatha and vipashyana are necessary.

Both shamatha meditation of natural resting
And vispashyana, which sees the unseeable,
Should not be separated but unified
In stillness, occurrence, and awareness.

On the basis of proper view, or ground mahamudra, one
practices path mahamudra. The core of the practice consists

in letting mind dwell in its natural freshness. This leads one to the realization that, by its very nature, the entire world of appearances is mahamudra. In order to let mind rest in its own nature, one practices shamatha meditation or mental calmness, and vipashyana or seeing the unseeable. In practicing shamatha, one should avoid the three types of errors (the three misunderstandings) mentioned earlier, and in vipashyana one should avoid the four strayings.

Shamatha

What should one know about shamatha, a form of meditation that involves letting the mind rest in itself? Mahamudra means being free from mental activities: mind rests in itself and one experiences ordinary mind. In order to do this, one first needs mental calmness. Why does one need mental calmness, if the idea is to experience ordinary mind? Since one is constantly distracted by external objects and sense perceptions, mind is unable to rest in its own nature even for an instant; this is why one must first overcome distraction. To avoid constant distraction, one practices mental calmness meditation and concentrates one-pointedly. Only when the mind is able to remain undistracted and calm can one rest in its nature.

There are many increasingly subtle techniques of shamatha meditation, that is, of letting mind rest in its own nature: meditation with a support, meditation without a support, and meditation on nature as such. The first form of shamatha meditation involves the use of a support. As long as one's awareness fixates on one object after another, mind is continually distracted. In order to take advantage of mind's tendency to fixate, one first practices shamatha meditation with a sense-object as support by placing an object in front of oneself either as a "general support" or as a "pure support." A general support might be a small stone or a piece of wood, whereas a pure support might be a likeness of the Buddha, such as a picture or a statue. Once one is familiar with this type of meditation, one can proceed with shamatha without a support.

Shamatha meditation without a support involves focusing on a mental representation, without resorting to an external or material object. This representation could be an image of the Buddha. First one should visualize certain details of appearance, such as the face, and then the entire figure. Once one is quite familiar with this method, then one can move on to shamatha meditation on nature as such.

The type of shamatha meditation that Jamgön Kongtrül Lodrö Thaye is referring to in this song is meditation on nature as such, the highest form of resting the mind. It involves letting mind rest in its own nature, without any object of concentration; if thoughts arise, one looks directly into their nature without suppressing or following them. In this way, thoughts disappear by themselves and one rests once again in the nature of mind.

This is expressed in the line of the Supplication to the Takpo Kagyüs that says: "The nature of thoughts is dharmakaya." Although thoughts arise from mind, their real nature is emptiness. Thoughts are the natural manifestation of mind; by looking at their nature, which is the nature of dharmakaya, or emptiness, one can see that they arise from mind and dissolve back into mind.

However, in our confusion, we regard our thoughts as real; we cling to our thoughts and follow them. But if instead of following our thoughts we look at their nature and see their emptiness, we are beholding the dharmakaya and thoughts melt back into the alaya-vijñana. The alaya-vijñana is like an ocean and the thoughts that arise in the mind are like waves. Ocean and waves are not separate from each other; waves are part of the ocean, they come out of it and return to it.

The purpose of this analogy is to explain how shamatha meditation is practiced in the mahamudra. One lets the mind rest in itself; if thoughts arise out of the ocean of the alaya-vijñana, one looks at their nature without either following or interrupting them. In this way thoughts dissolve back into mind like waves dissolving back into the ocean. If one practices in this manner, distractions or inner upheavals cannot arise. Resting in the nature of mind, that is, the nature of thoughts, is called shamatha meditation on nature as such, and is the highest form of meditation of mental calmness.

There are many ways to describe the states that one experiences in shamatha meditation. One way is to divide them into the so-called nine techniques of resting the mind, which one can read about in treatises on shamatha. Or they can also be described in accordance with the pith instructions, which present the experiences graphically. For instance, the first stage is compared with a roaring waterfall plunging down a cliff face; this stage corresponds to experiencing the upheavals of mind. At a later stage, mind is compared to a broad river, quieter and less turbulent. However, whether one follows the first or second explanation, the point is to achieve the actual fruition of shamatha meditation, which is physical and mental flexibility.

Because of negative karma and afflictive emotions, one often finds it difficult to do positive actions. One must therefore endeavor to cultivate positive thoughts and actions and avoid disturbing feelings. Flexibility in this context means overcoming not only the inability to act positively but also the struggle involved in doing so, until one achieves proper physical and mental conduct quite naturally and effortlessly. When one is free from afflictive emotions, proper behavior occurs spontaneously. Flexibility of mind and body is the ultimate fruition of mental calmness, at which point the experiences of joy, clarity, and nonconceptualization appear.

The experience of complete joy refers both to bodily sensations and to mental attitude. Any sense of heaviness disappears and one's body feels light and pleasant. This is similar to holding wool in one's hands—it feels nice and light. Mentally, one is full of joy and free from any form of dullness or distraction. Similarly, the experience of clarity also has a mental and physical component. It consists of a totally clear apprehension of sense perceptions, including the ability to distinguish the minutest details quite clearly.

The third experience, nonconceptualization is like experiencing space. Normally one thinks that things are the way one apprehends them. One hears sounds, sees forms, smells scents, and so on, and clings to these sense perceptions. One is caught up in the concept of the three times, the difference between male and female, and other dualities, and fixates on the characteristics that one attributes to phenomena. It is this particular form of fixation that nonconceptualization dissolves, giving one's experience the quality of space. One no longer fixates on the forms one sees, the sounds one hears, the concept of the three times, but instead one experiences space.

These three experiences of joy, clarity, and nonconceptualization occur mainly during meditation. During post-meditation one experiences everything as usual and fixates on the characteristics of phenomena. Only seldom do these three experiences occur outside of meditation.

Vipashyana

What does vipashyana, or seeing the unseeable, refer to? According to the teachings, vipashyana is "the wisdom which discriminates all phenomena," the insight that arises as the fruition of shamatha meditation. This does not mean, however, that vipashyana insight arises by itself out of the shamatha meditation of remaining in calmness.

In shamatha, one focuses the mind one-pointedly on something, whereas in vipashyana one experiences the actual nature of things. So vipashyana involves meditating on and investigating the nature of phenomena, or the fact that they have no real existence. Thus it can be said that shamatha is meditation by focusing, whereas vipashyana is meditation by analyzing. There are various ways of applying shamatha and vipashyana. For instance, one can first practice shamatha and then, once one has achieved mental calmness, proceed with vipashyana. Or else one can practice shamatha and vipashyana in alteration: first one practices shamatha meditation for a while, then one concentrates on developing vipashyana insight, after which one goes back to shamatha and then again back to vipashyana, and so on. Combining shamatha and vipashyana, calm-abiding and investigation, is an extremely effective method of practice.

If, for instance, one is concentrating on the coming and going of the breath during shamatha meditation, mental calmness means focusing totally on the breathing without letting the mind wander. Practicing vipashyana would mean that after a while one not only focuses on the breath alone but also examines and achieves insight into the nature of the breath. After one has turned one's mind for a while to the nature of the breath, then one concentrates again one-pointedly on the breathing. This is one way of alternating between shamatha and vipashyana practice. Although we speak about shamatha and vipashyana as two distinct types of meditation that can be practiced either sequentially or in alternation, the actual point is to join the two. If one practices only shamatha or vipashyana, then the unity of shamatha-vipashyana meditation will never arise.

What does it mean to practice shamatha and vipashyana together? Shamatha involves letting the mind rest on an object in a state of concentration. Both mind and object lack ultimate reality. This true nature is present at all times, not only when one achieves insight into it through vipashyana meditation. Maintaining this awareness or insight in shamatha meditation—that is, not separating one-pointedness from awareness—is the unity of shamatha and vipashyana.

When a feeling or thought arises, what does it mean to unite "calmness, movement, and awareness" through shamatha and vipashyana? Let us take the arising of anger as an example. First one notices that anger has arisen and acknowledges it. This corresponds to shamatha or mental calmness, that is, mindfulness which allows one to notice that a feeling has arisen. Based on this, one examines the feeling or thought by means of vipashyana. Calmness, movement, and awareness are the three phases that one examines. Calmness corresponds to the question: "where does the feeling or thought dwell?," movement to the question: "where does the feeling or thought go to?," and awareness to the question: "what is present between the arising and the subsiding of the thought or feeling?" This form of investigation brings one to the realization that the feeling has no real existence.

There is a widespread belief that shamatha and vipashyana are only practiced at the beginning of the path, as a sort of preliminary training prior to actual meditation. This is totally false, since both shamatha and vipashyana are practiced throughout the entire Buddhist path with all its different aspects. Thus shamatha can be found in the development of bodhichitta, the mind of enlightenment, as well as in the visualizations of the utpattikrama or development phase of vajrayana. These are nothing but a form of shamatha, even though different methods and concepts are being used. The same can be said for the six yogas of Naropa which involve, among other things, holding one's prana and meditating on the nadis and bindus. All these different forms of meditation are ways of practicing shamatha; they are based solely on mental calmness and cannot be practiced without it.

It is the same with vipashyana. On the shravaka path, vipashyana involves meditating on egolessness. On the bodhisattva path, it relates to meditating on emptiness and dependent origination as well as keeping in mind the fact that phenomena have no true existence. In the vajrayana, vipashyana is practiced in the sampannakrama or completion phase of meditation. There is no such thing as a Buddhist path that does not apply shamatha and vipashyana. This is why they are so important.

Beyond abandoning discursive confusion,
Beyond applying antidotes,
There will be a time when you spontaneously reach this.

If one practices shamatha and vipashyana properly, then there is no confusion and no discursive thoughts to be given up. When one looks at the nature of concepts, they disappear and dissolve into themselves, being by their very nature devoid of actual existence. Thus the application of specific antidotes against confusion becomes irrelevant. By simply letting the mind rest in its own nature, confusion dissolves spontaneously into itself with no need to apply antidotes.

When you have achieved realization,
There is nothing other than the meditative state.
At the threshold of freedom from loss and gain,
Even meditation does not exist.

When one realizes the ultimate nature of mind, there are no longer any moments that fall outside the sphere of meditation. However, the only way to achieve this realization is through meditation. One is free from the struggle to give up afflictive emotions or to "attain" wisdom. At this point, meditation as such no longer exists, because there is no longer any separation between meditator, meditation, and an object of meditation.

But for those beginners who are unable to dissolve the
*   hairline of conceptualization,*
Meditation is important.
When one practices meditation, there is experience.
This experience arises as the adornment of insight.

For beginners who have not yet overcome mental fixation meditation is necessary. As long as concepts are still present it is essential to practice meditation, otherwise the experiences of joy, clarity, and nonconcepualization will never arise. These experiences are called the "adornment of insight" because it is meditation that allows the insight into the nature of all phenomena to gradually arise.

This path is divided into the four yogas:

Shamatha meditation involves letting the mind dwell in its own nature; vipashyana is nondual insight into ultimate reality. By practicing the unity of shamatha and vipashyana one progressively achieves the four yogas.

The first yoga, one-pointedness, is the first glimpse of the nature of mind, the first experience of ordinary mind. If one keeps practicing, one achieves insight into the fact that the nature of mind is devoid of inherent reality. This is the second yoga, simplicity. By stabilizing this insight through meditation, one realizes that the entire phenomenal world is nothing else but the manifestation of one's own mind, or rather that mind is not different from external phenomena. This is the third yoga, one taste. By deepening this insight further through meditation, one realizes that there is no distinction or separation between meditation, meditator, and object of meditation. This is the fourth yoga, nonmeditation. Each of the four yogas is divided into three stages.

One-pointedness means recognizing the nature of mind;
Divided into the lesser, medium, and greater stages:
One sees the alternation of bliss and luminosity,
One masters resting in samadhi,
And experience continuously appears as luminosity.

The yoga of one-pointedness consists in recognizing the nature of mind after the teacher has pointed it out to one. According to the degree of stability achieved, three stages are distinguished within this first yoga: lesser, medium, and greater. As further insight into the nature of mind develops, the different experiences of meditation arise in alternation: bliss, clarity or luminosity, and nonthought. These in turn reinforce one's ability to rest in one's own mind, thus leading to greater mental depth. Because of one's ever-increasing awareness that phenomena are devoid of true existence, one's experience arises continuously as luminosity.

Simplicity means realizing the mind is without root;
Divided into the lesser, medium, and greater stages:
One realizes that the arising, ceasing, and dwelling are
*   empty,*
One is free from the ground and root of fixating on
*   appearance or emptiness,*
And one resolves the complexity of all dharmas.

On the level of the second yoga, simplicity, one recognizes not only that mind and dharmas are free from complexities, but also that they are devoid of actual inherent existence. This is insight into the meaning of reality. This stage of realization corresponds to the first bhumi on the bodhisattva path, the path of insight in mahayana. According to the stability of the realization, it is likewise divided into lesser, medium, and greater stages.

One realizes that mind is empty, free from arising, dwelling, and cessation. Through this insight, fixation on appearances and emptiness is dissolved. The habitual tendencies that lead one to separate the appearance of things from their emptiness disappear. By recognizing that there is no such thing as inherent existence, false views and doubts with regard to the mode of existence of inner and outer phenomena are resolved.

One taste means dissolving appearance and mind into each
*   other:*
Divided into the lesser, medium, and greater stages:
All dharmas of samsara and nirvana are dissolved into equal
*   taste.*

Appearance and mind become like water poured into water,
And from one taste, the various wisdoms arise.

The third yoga, one taste, is the union of external objects with the internal awareness that experiences them. Distinctions between subject and object no longer occur. This yoga is also divided into three stages, according to its level of stability.

All phenomena, that is, all external objects on which one fixates, as well as the awareness that apprehends them, are dissolved into equal taste—there is no longer any separation between them. In the same way, appearance and mind also become inseparable like water poured into water. One realizes that all appearances are the innate manifestation of mind and thus not separate from mind. The experience of one taste arising from insight into the oneness of samsara and nirvana leads to the various types of wisdom.

Nonmeditation means the utter exhaustion of conceptual
      mind;
Divided into the lesser, medium, and greater stages:
One is free from meditation and meditator,
The habitual patterns of primitive beliefs about reality are
      gradually cleared away,
And the mother and son luminosity dissolve together.
The wisdom of dharmadhatu extends throughout space.

On the level of the fourth yoga, nonmeditation, all concepts and ideas disappear and all notions about meditation and meditator are completely resolved. Once again, this yoga is divided into three stages in accordance with the degree of stability of the realization.

First, one realizes that there is no distinction between

meditation and meditator. Conceptual obscurations are purified and one attains "threefold purity" free from concepts. Using generosity as an example, this means that one is free from the idea of a giver, a receiver, and a gift. One is free from the notion that these three are separate from each other.

What does the expression "mother and son luminosity" refer to? Because of one's confusion one is not ready to recognize ultimate nature at the outset. However, by practicing path mahamudra on the basis of the proper view achieved through ground mahamudra, then the "son" —each individual experience on the path—comes ever closer to the "mother" —true reality, until the insight acquired and reality become one, which is the meeting of mother and son, and one achieves the all-pervasive wisdom of dharmadhatu.

In short, in meditation:
One-pointedness means that mind is still as long as one
    wishes,
Seeing the very nature of ordinary mind.
Simplicity means the realization of groundlessness.
One taste means liberating
All possible dualistic fixations through insight.
Nonmeditation means transcending all sophistries of
    meditation and nonmeditation,
The exhaustion of habitual patterns.

Normally, mind is constantly distracted and churned up, even in meditation. Thoughts arise and disappear, new thoughts arise and disappear in turn, and mind cannot rest on one point. As long as one does not recognize the nature of mind, one experiences a separation between mind and thoughts. This is why one has the idea that, in shamatha meditation, there is "someone" who is holding the mind in focus. As long as one has not recognized the nature of thoughts, these disturb the mind. However, if one has understood the nature of mind—and thus the nature of thoughts—then mind can always rest in itself, without ever being affected or distracted by that which arises within the mind. One experiences ordinary mind, that is, one sees the nature of mind and understands that mind is no different from the present moment of awareness. This is why this yoga is called one-pointedness.

Explanations of mind similar to this vajra doha can also be found in another text by Jamgön Kongtrül Lodrö Thaye. That text states that one should contemplate the basis of mind and realize that it is nothing other than the present moment of awareness, the thought of nowness. One should not look for mind elsewhere. When one contemplates mind or the nature of thoughts, then the object contemplated and the subject contemplating become one, since mind itself is looking at mind. Because the nature of mind is emptiness, there is nothing that is seen, no object. However, instead of experiencing mere nothingness, one experiences luminosity.

If one looks into the nature of thoughts, then these dissolve into themselves and luminosity arises, the inherent luminosity and awareness of mind itself. These two aspects of mind—emptiness and luminosity—are inseparable from each other and are actually one. This is the nature of mind. Looking into the nature of mind is nothing other than experiencing the present moment of awareness and seeing that there is no mind outside this present moment of awareness. This experience is given different names according to the tradition describing it. In the mahamudra tradition, it is known as the experience of ordinary mind, whereas in maha ati it is called awareness. However, both of these terms designate the experience of the nowness of mind.

From the point of view of ordinary mind, thoughts are no longer things to be suppressed or cultivated. By experiencing momentary thoughts directly one also experiences their nature, that is, their emptiness, self-awareness, and self-luminosity. There is no separation between the experiencer looking into the nature of thoughts and the experience, the thoughts themselves. The experience of dharmakaya is nothing other than letting the mind rest in this state. One realizes that wisdom or dharmakaya is not something external to be gained. Rather, it is a matter of resting in a state of oneness, of experiencing and recognizing the present moment of awareness.

However, this is easier said than done. As long as one is bound to the concept of duality and makes a distinction between the subject who is contemplating the mind and the mind itself, one cannot recognize this moment. In order to do so, it is essential to accumulate merit and purify oneself of obscurations. Notwithstanding the saying that "Buddha is in the palm of one's hand"—that is, that what one is looking for is to be found nowhere but in oneself—unless one strives to accumulate merit and purify oneself of one's obscurations, one will never realize this. This is why preliminary practices, accumulation of merit, purification of obscurations, yidam practices, and so on, are so important. They are practiced in order to bring one to the point where this realization is possible.

Everyone has the ability to achieve this realization. It is not only very near, it is actually within oneself. However, it is up to each person to work toward it. Buddha is not outside oneself. This realization, apart from which there is no enlightenment, is the actual meaning of practice, the ultimate path of mahamudra and maha ati.

By deepening one's meditation through further practice, one achieves the second yoga, simplicity. This involves realizing that there is no difference between mind itself and that which is investigated in mind.

When one understands this correctly, the fixation on the separation between apprehended object and apprehending awareness disappears. One realizes that all phenomena are none other than a manifestation or expression of mind, and recognizes the oneness of mind and appearances. This is one taste, the third yoga.

Once mind and appearances have dissolved into one taste, there is no longer any difference between meditation and nonmeditation. These are concepts that are useful only on a superficial level. The conceptual and subtle obscurations of habitual patterns are removed and the separation between meditator and meditation disappears. This is known as reaching the dharmakaya kingdom of nonmeditation.

In this way, from the great lords of yogins,
Naropa and Maitripa,
Down to the lord guru Padma Wangchen,
The golden garland of the Kagyüs
Reached the dharmakaya kingdom of nonmeditation,
Spontaneously cleared away the darkness of the two
    obscurations,
Expanded the great power of the two knowledges,
Opened the treasury of benefit for the sake of others
    pervading space, . . .

All the teachers in the golden garland of the Kagyü transmission—from Tilopa and Naropa down to Situ Pema

Nyinje Wangpo, Jamgön Kongtrül Lodrö Thaye's teacher, and from the latter down to the sixteenth Gyalwa Karmapa, Rangjung Rigpe Dorje—have used mahamudra to achieve the dharmakaya kingdom of nonmeditation and transmitted the mahamudra lineage, the lineage of realization, in an unbroken line from teacher to disciple. They have overcome both emotional and conceptual obscurations and accomplished the twofold wisdom of depth and vastness. The wisdom of depth is recognizing the actual nature of all phenomena, their emptiness, and the wisdom of vastness is simultaneously seeing the luminosity of all phenomena, their unobstructed manifestation on a relative plane. The Kagyü lineage holders not only understand the meaning of mahamudra, they also act on their knowledge. With a motivation of loving-kindness and concern for the welfare of all beings, they strive to help beings attain enlightenment, like a person who puts a treasure at the disposal of others.

And remained in the refuge of mind free from doubt.

Because of the pefect qualities of the holders of the mahamudra lineage, it is possible for all beings to place their trust in them as a refuge, with the certainty that one will be protected in this and future lives, beyond any doubt and insecurity.

The Kagyü lineage is known to be passed from one to
*   another.*
It is known not by words alone, but by their meaning.

The mahamudra lineage of realization is passed down from teacher to disciple and so on down the line. Thus each one rests on the previous one. It is not just an empty formula. In actual fact, not only the words, but also the recognition and inspiration of realization are transmitted from one to another, from teacher to disciple, thus giving rise to the ocean of siddhas.

Please guide even such a lowborn savage as myself,
Who possesses the merest mark of your noble lineage,
Quickly to the kingdom of nonmeditation.
Kind one, please utterly exhaust my conceptual mind.

Jamgön Kongtrül Lodrö Thaye is directing his request to the Kagyü lineage in general, and in particular to his own teacher Situ Pema Nyinje Wangpo. Claiming to possess only "the merest mark" of their noble lineage, as opposed to its true meaning, he requests the Kagyü lineage to grant him the inspiration that will enable him to exhaust promptly the confusion of conceptual mind in order to experience the dharmakaya kingdom of nonmeditation.

Summary of Path Mahamudra
Path mahamudra means applying practice to the path of mahamudra, based on the proper view acquired through ground mahamudra. It is necessary first of all to understand the nature of mind properly: by its very nature, one's own mind is dharmakaya itself, and relative appearances are the inherent manifestation of dharmakaya, its luminosity. In order to consolidate this insight, one accomplishes the various practices of the path of mahamudra: mahamudra-style shamatha and vipashyana, as well as utpattikrama and sampannakrama in the vajrayana, including meditation on prana, nadi, and bindu.

The core of mahamudra meditation involves resting in the present moment of awareness without either altering, creating, or suppressing anything. Path mahamudra means remaining undistracted in the freshness of thoughts, relaxing without meditating on anything and resting calmly in the primordial unfabricated state. Composure and awareness are essential to achieve this. Composure is needed to focus the mind and bring it to rest, whereas awareness is needed to perceive coarse and subtle thoughts or distractions of the mind. In maintaining composure and awareness, one should be neither too tight nor too loose, since this would give rise respectively to wildness and dullness of mind.

FRUITION MAHAMUDRA

The fruition mahamudra is spoken of like this:
The ground is receiving the transmission of the innate
*   trikaya;*
The path is applying the key points of the view and
*   meditation;*
The fruition is the actualization of the stainless trikaya.

Fruition mahamudra is the realization that relative appearances and mind are, by their very nature, the three kayas. To achieve this realization it is absolutely essential first of all to have a clear understanding of the ground, the proper view. Dharmakaya is the fact that whether one is talking about relative external appearances or the internal mechanisms of mind, by their very nature these are devoid of true existence. Sambhogakaya means that manifestation is unobstructed, and nirmanakaya that appearances are numerous and manifold. In the same way that dharmakaya is inherent in mind, the light of dharmakaya is inherent in appearances. Mind and appearances are as inseparable as the light of dharmakaya and its rays. These are the key points of the view.

As the Mahamudra Prayer of the third Karmapa, Omniscient Rangjung Dorje, says:

> If one looks at things, nothing is present, and one sees
> them as mind;
> If one looks at mind, there is no mind, it is by its very
> essence empty;
> If one looks at both, one is self-liberated from the fixation
> on duality.
> May we recognize luminosity, the nature of our minds.

If one looks at objects, that is, external phenomena, and one has some understanding of their ultimate nature, one can realize that objects are not truly, permanently, and unchangingly present, but are mere mental images—it is mind which identifies them as one thing or another. If one looks at the nature of mind, one can see only the present moment of awareness or thoughts; other than this one experiences no mind. One sees the nature of mind, its emptiness, its lack of true existence.

Phenomena are not truly present, but are merely projections of a mind which itself has no true existence; the appearance of phenomena is based on mind's luminosity. When one recognizes these two aspects, fixation on duality—the separation between external appearances and internally fixating mind—dissolves into itself. There is nothing to reject and nothing to attain and one recognizes mind's luminosity, its ultimate nature.

Ground mahamudra introduces one to the proper view, that is, to the unity of appearance and mind, the trikaya. On this basis, one practices the path, the application of the view of meditation.

In terms of meditation, by practicing shamatha and vipashyana, mind rests spontaneously in the experience of nonduality, the unity of appearance and mind. One realizes that mind is dharmakaya and appearances are the manifestation of dharmakaya, its light rays. In terms of action, one adopts the conduct of a bodhisattva who has understood emptiness and compassion. This conduct reinforces meditative experiences and hastens fruition. This is the path of view, meditation, and action; the practice of these three leads to fruition, the actualization of the stainless trikaya.

Therefore, its essence is emptiness, simplicity, dharmakaya.
Its manifestation is the luminous nature of sambhogakaya.
Its strength, manifold and unceasing, is nirmanakaya.
This is the sovereign of all reality.

Basic nature is devoid of true existence, since it is empty and free from extremes: this is dharmakaya. Out of dharmakaya or emptiness, free from extremes, appearances manifest unobstructedly. This is the luminous nature of sambhogakaya. Out of the unobstructed luminosity arise the manifold manifestations of the nirmanakaya. Therefore, the three kayas—dharmakaya, sambhogakaya, and nirmanakaya—pervade everything. There is nothing that lies outside their scope, nothing that does not partake of their nature.

The nature of mahamudra is unity,
The realm of dharmas free from accepting or rejecting.

The three kayas are not separate from each other. When one actualizes the dharmadhatu, the realm of phenomena, the unity of the three kayas, there is no longer any distinction between samsara as a state of confusion to be given up and nirvana as liberation to be attained. In the unchangeable realm of dharmas this distinction no longer holds.

Possessing the beauty of unconditioned bliss,
It is the great and vast wealth of wisdom.
It is the natural form of kindness transcending thought.

Dharmadhatu, the spontaneous unity of the three kayas, is the stainless great bliss, the unity of skillful means and compassion in the vastness of unobstructed, all-pervasive supreme wisdom. Out of the unity of these two aspects, the unconditioned great bliss of experiences and the depth of wisdom, the active kindness of all buddhas and bodhisattvas manifests.

Thus, the state of omniscience is not a mere nothingness, a total void, but rather the wealth of perfect wisdom. The inherent expression of this wealth of wisdom is the kindness of all the buddhas and bodhisattvas that reaches all beings without obstruction. This kindness cannot be conceptualized, it is beyond any concepts one may have about it.

Through prajña, it does not dwell in samsara.
Through karuna, it does not dwell in nirvana.
Through effortlessness, buddha activity is spontaneously
* accomplished.*

Having achieved perfect wisdom, the understanding of emptiness, the person who has actualized mahamudra is not caught up in samsara — the three spheres of conditioned existence — but rather experiences threefold purity. Having also realized perfect compassion, the accomplishment of skillful means, he or she does not dwell in a one-sided nirvana, a state of mere rest, the state that is achieved by the shravakas and pratyekabuddhas in their efforts to attain personal liberation. Out of the unity of wisdom and great, all-pervasive compassion, buddha activity for the benefit of beings is effortlessly and spontaneously accomplished.

The luminosity of ground and path, mother and son, dissolve
    together.
The ground and fruition embrace one another.
Buddha is discovered in one's mind:
The wish-fulfilling treasure overflows within.
E ma! How wonderful and marvelous!

The ground, the true nature of phenomena, and the experiences accumulated along the path dissolve together. As has already been explained, this is described in terms of the meeting of mother and sun, the luminosity of the ground and the fruition of the path become one. This is the actualization of one's own innate nature. Thus, enlightenment is not something new that one acquires, nor is it found outside oneself—like traveling to a foreign country—but consists simply of recognizing the nature of one's own mind. Having recognized one's own mind and attained enlightenment, a treasure opens up inside oneself, for this attainment enables one to act for the benefit of all beings. It is truly wonderful and marvelous to have discovered Buddha in one's own mind and to have opened the wish-fulfilling treasure within.

Since in the view of mahamudra
Analysis does not apply,
Cast mind-made knowledge far away.
Since in the meditation on mahamudra
There is no way of fixating on a thought,
Abandon deliberate meditation.

Since in the action of mahamudra
There is no reference point for any action,
Be free from the intention to act or not.
Since in the fruition of mahamudra
There is no attainment to newly acquire,
Cast hopes, fears, and desires away.

The view of mahamudra does not involve thinking that
mahamudra or mind are one thing or another, nor does mahamudra meditation involve analyzing thoughts. While
mind rests in itself, one sees the nature of thoughts directly
and realizes that there is no arising, cessation, or dwelling.
Therefore, one should cast away mind-made representations about one's possible mental makeup and simply rest
in the nature of mind. This is the view of mahamudra.

Mahamudra meditation should be free from any form of
fixation on meditation. One should not think, "Now I am
meditating . . . this is meditation . . . this is not meditation."
Free from any such ideas about meditation and without deliberately placing the mind in any fabricated state, one
should just let the mind rest in itself. Mahamudra action is
free from concepts such as "I will do this, I will not do that."
This is freedom from the intention to act or not.

We have seen that the path of mahamudra leads to a fruition that is not something that one must acquire anew. Since
attainment is not something one lacks and must therefore
obtain, one should cast away all hopes, fears, and desires
that, in one's ignorance, one may have with regard to attainment. Notions such as "If I practice this, I will attain
that and if I do not practice it, I will not attain it," are unnecessary.

Summary of the View, Meditation, and Action of Mahamudra

From an absolute point of view, there is no difference between samsara and nirvana. However, not having recognized the nature of one's own mind, one is under the impression that samsara and nirvana are two separate states and is therefore subject to confusion.

As is said in the Mahamudra Prayer of the third Karmapa:

Inherent appearance, which has never existed, is
  misconstrued as an object.
Due to ignorance, inherent awareness is misconstrued as
  ego.
Because of fixation on duality, one wanders in the round of
  rebirths.
May ignorance, the root of confusion, be overcome.

Confusion arises because on the one hand one does not recognize that external objects are the inherent manifestation of one's mind and takes these objects to be real and, on the other hand, because one misapprehends the emptiness of one's mind and takes it to be an ego. This duality leads to the distinction between "I" and "other," between samsara and nirvana, even though this distinction does not apply on an ultimate level. The view of mahamudra enables one to understand that samsara and nirvana are not separate entities, that there is neither an object to be apprehended nor apprehending awareness.

Mahamudra meditation involves letting one's mind rest in its primordial unfabricated state, without making any distinctions between object and experiencing awareness. Mahamudra action consists in practicing the conduct of a bodhisattva based on the unobstructed strength that arises from the unity of emptiness and compassion. By actualizing these three aspects of the path—view, meditation, and action—one recognizes the ultimate nature of reality, the unity of samsara and nirvana or fruition mahamudra.

This is the depth of the mind of all Kagyüs.
It is the only path on which the victorious ones and their
        sons journey.
Theirs is the upaya that reverses the vicious circle of
        existence
And the dharma that brings enlightenment in one life.
Here is the essence of the teachings, sutras, and tantras.

Mahamudra is the attainment of the mahasiddhas, the innumerable Kagyü teachers. All the victorious ones and their sons—that is, all the buddhas and bodhisattvas—of the three times and the ten directions have attained enlightenment by following this path. The confusion of the three realms of samsara is eliminated thanks to the path of mahamudra that enables one to achieve buddhahood, the state of Vajradhara, in one lifetime. Mahamudra is the essence of all the teachings of Buddha, the sutras, and tantras.

May I and all sentient beings prevading space
Together attain the simultaneity of realization and
        liberation.
And attain supreme mahamudra.

Jamgön Kongtrül Lodrö Thaye composed this doha when he himself had attained the realization of mahamudra. In this vajra song he expresses inner experience that can be understood by anyone, rather than requiring lofty intellectual knowledge.

··· *Commentary* ···

On the one hand, this doha is quite complicated, certain passages and concepts being somewhat difficult to understand; on the other, it encompasses the entire path. There is nothing that is not contained in it, from the ground to the ultimate fruition. For this reason it is extremely beneficial to practice in accordance with this doha. By doing so, may all beings quickly attain the highest realization of mahamudra!

QUESTIONS AND ANSWERS

STUDENT: How does confusion arise?

RINPOCHE: Confusion has no beginning, since as such it does not exist; this is beginningless samsara. The same is true also for the end of confusion. On the one hand, confusion has no end, since it does not exist; on the other hand, one can actually put an end to it in the sense of liberating oneself from the state of confusion. This is called "putting an end to samsara."

S: Can one fall back into confusion after having reached enlightenment?

R: No, because enlightenment involves being free from ignorance. However, enlightenment is not the end of confusion, even though it is described as such, since ultimately there is no confusion, ignorance, or samsara from which to liberate oneself. The reason we talk about putting an end to samsara is because the cause for suffering has been overcome.

S: How can confusion arise, if mind has always been empty and luminous?

R: Confusion involves not recognizing the nature of mind. Although the nature of mind is perfectly pure and clear, we experience confusion as long as mind has not recognized its own nature.

S: Are there beings who have always been enlightened, without ever having followed the path?
R: No, everyone must follow the path. The only factor that varies is the amount of time that different beings require to achieve realization.

S: It seems to me that the path to enlightenment is really quite long and difficult.
R: Achieving enlightenment means recognizing one's own mind. What is at stake is whether one recognizes the nature of one's mind or not. However, getting to the point where this recognition is possible takes a long time because habitual patterns are very deeply rooted in our minds, in our alaya-vijñana.

S: How can one develop the proper view with regard to relative and ultimate truth?
R: There are basically two ways of achieving the proper view: one is to learn the proper view theoretically and the other is to discover through one's meditation. Of these two, the first is easier. In addition, having the proper view is a tremendous aid for one's meditation. In this context, meditation means shamatha and vipashyana—meditating on the nature of mind.

Personally, I find it best to develop first the proper view through theory. This does not mean that one should learn the entire Buddhist philosophy. It is desirable to study the view theoretically while concurrently practicing shamatha or another form of meditation, because theory alone is useless beyond a certain point. Only meditation is really effective.

S: Doesn't appropriating a point of view reinforce conceptual thinking?

R: Yes, to some extent it does. This is why it is extremely important to combine study and practice. Buddha Shakyamuni himself said that one should not rely on words alone, but should experience their meaning.

S: Do the experiences of bliss, clarity, and nonthought as well as the experience of emptiness depend on the techniques used on the path?

R: Although these experiences depend somewhat on the meditation techniques used, they depend mainly on the individual practitioner—whether the practitioner is oriented toward experiencing bliss or emptiness.

S: Does nonthought mean that no thoughts arise?

R: Although the experiences of bliss, luminosity, and nonthought are experienced during shamatha meditation, they are only a side-effect of shamatha and not its actual fruition. Nonthought means that one's fixation on various experiences and sense perceptions like hearing, tasting, and so on, is transformed. Instead of feeling separate from one's experience, one feels increasingly at one with it. One has a sense of all-pervasive space. Thoughts do occur, of course, but one does not cling to them. It never happens that no thoughts arise at all.

The fruition of shamatha, and also of vipashyana, is flexibility and lightness, in the sense that one is in touch with everything—body, speech, and mind. Normally what happens is that even if we want to act positively, our emotions prevent us from orienting our minds in the right direction. Flexibility and lightness means that we have a sense of inner space that allows us to act the way we would really like, without being carried away by our emotional upheavals.

S: What is the difference between alaya-vijñana and the nature of mind?

R: Alaya-vijñana is the basis for experiencing confusion. Concepts and thoughts collect in the alaya-vijñana and later come up to the surface. The nature of mind is emptiness, its quality is luminosity; together they constitute a unity.

S: What role does the alaya-vijñana play in the arising of confusion?

R: Through the sense consciousness of seeing, for instance, a form is grasped; mind consciousness evaluates the perception and the seventh consciousness deposits the imprint created by this evaluation in the alaya-vijñana. Through habitual patterns that are reinforced in the alaya-vijñana, disturbing emotions arise; this is called the cloudy mind.

S: I can't imagine these habitual patterns that are deposited in the alaya-vijñana.

R: Impressions and habitual patterns arise as follows: We live in duality because we believe in "I" and "other." Out of that arise conflicting emotions that condition our actions of body, speech, and mind. These actions, or actually the imprint they leave behind or the behavioral tendencies they create, are placed in the alaya-vijñana by the seventh consciousness. If the proper conditions come together, the impressions deposited in the alaya-vijñana are activated; they ripen and are experienced again. This is what is meant by habit—when we are in the habit of doing something, we do it automatically, without having to think about it. However, if we have not acquired a particular habit, then we must think before acting; we have to make an effort, because we cannot act automatically.

S: So everything we do automatically is based on habitual patterns?

R: Yes, one could say so. However, it is important to take into account the intensity of the habitual pattern, including karmic tendencies. Some of our habitual patterns do not stem from this life alone, and patterns formed in previous lifetimes are stronger than the ones formed in this life.

S: In the sevenfold service, one requests the buddhas not to pass into a one-sided nirvana, so to speak. What is meant by this type of nirvana? Is it even possible for a buddha to pass into a one-sided nirvana?

R: This request is addressed to the buddhas and bodhisattvas of the ten directions and the three times. From the point of view of the present, there are buddhas who have already passed into nirvana, and others who intend to do so. Buddhas are always working limitlessly for the benefit of beings and have the ability to manifest in countless bodies. However, from the point of view of sentient beings, it is necessary to establish a connection. For this, we need a reference point, and this is exactly what this prayer provides. In order to create this connection, we address this request to the buddhas, as a sort of reference point. The term nirvana has two meanings. The first meaning refers to a state that lies beyond both samsara and nirvana—a state in which there is no longer any separation between samsara and nirvana and both are experienced as one. The other meaning, the one referred to here, is nirvana as a state in which the form kayas dissolve into the dharmakaya. Developing bodhichitta produces limitless benefit for beings. A person who has realized emptiness is able to work for the benefit of beings in one or more bodies.

S: What are the sixty-four qualities of a buddha?

R: These sixty-four qualities are divided into thirty-two qualities that are exclusive attributes of a buddha, and thirty-two qualities of ripening. One can also say that buddhas possess limitless qualities, since these sixty-four qualities include all the qualities that can possibly exist.

S: What are the eight qualities of Vajradhara?

R: First, Vajradhara does not have an ordinary body. He is dharmakaya, the unity of emptiness and luminosity. His bodily form is not made of flesh and blood or any other material substance. Even though he appears, his nature is emptiness.

Second, even though he is empty by his very nature, he manifests unobstructedly in his form: as sambhogakaya, blue in color, with crossed wrists, holding a vajra and a ghanta in his hands, and with all the other attributes. This is unobstructed appearance.

Third, he possesses all of the qualities of a buddha, that is, the thirty-two qualities and the eighty special attributes.

Fourth, dharmakaya Vajradhara pervades all of samsara and nirvana. There is nothing that is not pervaded by him. Although he possesses a body, he is not limited to this body but pervades everything to the same extent.

Fifth, Vajradhara's dharmakaya body does not cast a shadow.

Sixth, he is independent of light and darkness and free from any stains whatsoever.

Seventh, to symbolize the unwavering aspect of dharmakaya, Vajradhara's body is the color of an autumn sky, deep blue.

Eighth, he possesses omniscience with regard to the three times—past, present, and future—without establishing any distinctions among these concepts, the way we do. To symbolize this, his eyes always remain unchangeable in the same position.

S: What does *luminosity* mean? Should we understand it symbolically?

R: What is actually meant by *luminosity* is the aspect of unobstructedness—because of emptiness everything is possible, everything can arise unobstructedly and endlessly in each moment. It does not refer to sunlight or artificial light.

S: What does *the unobstructedness of mind* refer to?

R: Mind is unobstructed because it is empty by its very nature. In all regards it is perfect emptiness. Since mind is emptiness, it is in itself unobstructed, everything can arise. If this were not the case, emptiness would amount to mere negation, the extreme of nihilism.

S: What is the meaning of the line: "On the threshold of nonduality there is nowhere to dwell"?

R: The arising of mind and phenomena is only true from a relative point of view; ultimately, by their very nature, they are unoriginated, or nonexistent. However, they are not nothingness, but rather manifest unceasingly. These two aspects, that is, the unoriginatedness on the ultimate plane and the unceasing continuity on the relative plane, cannot be distinguished from each other. This is what is meant by freedom from arising, cessation, and dwelling.

Mind and the phenomenal world are ultimately unoriginated. However, one could conclude from this that they are devoid of continuity. This is not the case—on the contrary, continuity is unobstructed and everything comes into manifestation constantly. Mind experiences the totality of samsara and nirvana. Since mind has not arisen and has no end, there can obviously be nowhere to dwell. Thus, the nature of mind is free from arising, cessation, and dwelling.

S: Although mind is free from arising, cessation, and dwelling, do all other phenomena nevertheless arise by virtue of their impermanence?

R: On a relative plane, everything—not only external phenomena but also mind—comes into existence and ceases to exist, since thoughts are constantly arising and disappearing. However, ultimately, neither mind nor phenomena arise.

S: What type of meditation is most used to develop mindfulness?

R: All forms of meditation aim at developing mindfulness. Often, one begins with shamatha and *tonglen*—giving and taking—in order to develop bodhichitta. Also, in the vajrayana, the point of all the yidam visualizations, including both utpatti- and sampannakrama, is to stabilize awareness. For instance, if one practices the utpattikrama by concentrating on the form of the yidam, mental quietude or shamatha develops naturally.

S : If one is having difficulties with one's *ngöndro*, should one practice it nonetheless?

R : Although other practices are fine, ngöndro is extremely useful. You can see this by comparing the different Buddhist paths. On the sutrayana path of causes and conditions you need three endless kalpas to accumulate merit. However, on the vajrayana path there are extraordinary methods like ngöndro practice that can be used to accumulate merit in an extremely short time. For this reason it is very important to practice ngöndro. Even if one cannot do prostrations because of physical impairments, it is still important to practice taking refuge, Vajrasattva mantra, and so on. Among the preliminary practices, guruyoga is especially important. This is because in the path of mahamudra, one's teacher's blessings are essential in order for ultimate wisdom to unfold.

S : Can one practice Vajrasattva mantra without having done prostrations?

R : Yes, if one is sick. Otherwise, one should do all the practices one after the other.

S : On the one hand, we are told that we contain buddhanature within ourselves and that it is unnecessary to purify the nature of our minds. On the other, preliminary practices are a form of purification. Is this not contradictory?

R : It is true that all qualities are totally present in one's buddha-nature. However, we are unable to realize this as long as our habitual tendencies prevent us from doing so. In order to liberate ourselves from our habitual tendencies we need both to purify ourselves from our obscurations and evil deeds and also to accumulate merit and wisdom. Only the merit and wisdom that we accumulate through ngöndro can enable us to recognize our inherent qualities.

S : What are the three gates of liberation?
R : The three gates of liberation refer to ground, path, and fruition. Ground is free from arising, path is free from characteristics, and fruition is free from desire and struggle. Ground in this case refers to the proper view which we have already described—namely, that all phenomena ultimately have neither beginning nor end, and are therefore free from dwelling. The path is the approach to this realization. Since there is nothing on which one can meditate, that is, nothing which distinguishes the path, the path does not have any distinctive characteristics and involves simply dwelling in the original nature of mind. Fruition is free from desire and struggle. It is the realization that ultimately there is no fruition that one could possibly attain. It is also freedom from the insecurity of thinking that one will not attain this fruition.

S : What are the three types of thoughts?
R : Subtle, tangible, and coarse. However, thoughts themselves are none of these three. It is our fixation on thoughts that creates the difference in intensity. This is why we distinguish three types of thought. For instance, conflicting emotions that create intense upheavals are considered coarse thoughts, whereas subtle thoughts are those that arise during shamatha meditation but hardly disturb or distract one at all. They simply dissolve immediately after having arisen. Through meditation on mental quietude we can gradually resolve our fixation on thoughts.

S : To me, dissolving thoughts seems easy, but what about bodily pains?

R: It depends mainly on one's own practice. We are extremely attached to our bodies, which is why it is so difficult to transmute bodily pain. One can begin by first looking at the nature of the sensation or pain when minor aches or ailments arise. This is a very good way of dealing with them, but it requires a certain amount of experience in this type of practice. If one practices consistently for a long time, then one will eventually be able to deal with stronger pains in the same way. However, it is difficult because we are so attached to our bodies. Another very good alternative is to develop bodhichitta and take on all the pain of sentient beings by wishing that their pain be gathered in one's own.

S: Does everybody possess a particular karmic connection to a given teacher?

R: No, they do not. This is why we talk about having a "root guru." This expression designates the teacher who is able to ripen and free the mental continuum of a given student. This is the characteristic of the root guru that a student should be on the lookout for. In some teacher-student relationships there is already a karmic connection from previous lifetimes because the student had made intense aspiration prayers. It is also possible that the teacher may not need any words to introduce the student to mahamudra but can do so through symbols or in other ways.

S: It is said that vajrayana is a means for attaining enlightenment in one lifetime. Does this not contradict the kalpa-long connection to a guru which you mentioned?

R: In general, one does need a kalpa-long connection with a teacher in order to achieve the state of Vajradhara, the state of oneness, in this lifetime. Then, if one comes into contact with the vajrayana teachings in this lifetime, one can achieve enlightenment in an instant on being introduced to the nature of mind because of one's longstanding connection with one's teacher.

Let us suppose that in this lifetime someone has access to the vajrayana teachings and meets a teacher with whom he or she already has a longstanding connnection. By simply following the teacher's instructions, that person will realize the nature of mind and attain enlightenment either in this lifetime or in the near future, that is, in the bardo or in the following lives. It depends on one's individual karma. It is said that one will attain buddhahood in sixteen lifetimes at the most. The seed of enlightenment has been planted in one's mind and is ever closer to ripening.

S: What does *abhisheka* mean?

R: As a rule, vajrayana abhishekas, also called initiations or empowerments, aim at ripening the mind of the student. An abhisheka is made up of several sections each of which is actually a separable abhisheka. Basically, there are four. The first is the abhisheka of body, the "vase abhisheka," that purifies all the obscurations of body. By ripening the body, it leads to the realization of nirmanakaya. The second is the abhisheka of speech, or "secret abhisheka," that purifies obscurations of speech and leads to the realization of sambhogakaya. The third is the abhisheka of mind, the "wisdom-awareness abhisheka." It introduces the student to the wisdom of bliss and emptiness, the fruition of which is the realization of dharmakaya. The fourth abhisheka is the so-called "word abhiseka," the actual preparation for mahamudra, the introduction into the nature of mind. Through this section of the abhisheka, body, speech, and mind are ripened simultaneously. Its fruition is the realization of the oneness of the three kayas, or svabhavikakaya.

S: Can one learn to have trust and devotion?

R: First one should develop trust, based on which devotion can develop. Briefly, trust means being certain that something is right, whether it is the teacher or the teachings—not just as a mere thought, but as inner conviction. You trust the Buddha or your teacher when you are sure that they are perfect and that they can really help you. Based on this trust, devotion blazes. Although devotion can have different degrees of intensity, it is always a stronger inner experience than trust. Real, unfabricated devotion consists of seeing the teacher as a perfect buddha.

Trust is like a container into which one can pour something. It is also like a seed that can grow into a plant and bear fruit. If the seed is burnt, no fruit will come out of it. Similarly, according to the Buddha, it is impossible to practice the path of dharma if there is no trust. You do not simply place your trust in something. Rather, trust arises beause one first listens to the dharma, thinks about the contents of the teachings, and develops faith in their rightness. This leads to trust in the teachings and the teacher. Initially, developing trust requires an effort. However, the more you practice, the more trust becomes something natural, that grows organically.

To sum up, trust involves having certainty in the teaching and the teacher—being convinced that they possess the ability to show you the right path. Once trust is established, then devotion can unfold. Traditionally it is said that when you feel devotion, tears well up in your eyes and you get goose bumps and other signs. Finally, devotion comes forth spontaneously, by itself.

S: What is the relationship between utpatti- and sampannakrama meditation in the vajrayana and mahamudra meditation?

R: Although mahamudra meditation does not have an object on which one meditates, this does not mean that one meditates on nothing at all—the object, so to speak, is the state free from extremes, free from fixation on the experiencer. Whereas in utpatti- and sampannakrama meditations of the vajrayana one is meditating on the unity of luminosity and emptiness. Ultimately, they are the same.

These explanations make mahamudra sound extremely easy, but actually practitioners generally find the practice of mahamudra meditation quite difficult. The reason for all the difficulties is because we are attached to so many things. This is why the vajrayana path is divided into several stages, utpattikrama and sampannakrama, or development and completion stages. These are the special skillful means of the vajrayana. Utpattikrama prevents you from falling into the extreme of nihilism, whereas sampannakrama helps you overcome fixation on the reality of the phenomenal world. Ultimately, when both of these aspects are united, you transcend extreme views and reach the state of simplicity with regard to the mode of existence of phenomena. In order to attain this realization it is very important to practice the utpattikrama properly, for instance by being aware of the real meaning of the visualizations, which is to bring all impure experiences to a pure plane, and also by understanding the symbolism of each and every detail and not limiting oneself to practicing on only one quality.

S: What is the difference between sutra and tantra mahamudra?

R: In sutra mahamudra, the emptiness aspect is stressed as an "object" of meditation—the emptiness of phenomena, free both from extreme modes of existence and from any notions the experiencer may have about them. Whereas in tantra mahamudra the luminosity aspect—the skillful means—is highlighted. In spite of this difference, the goal is the same. By realizing the unity of bliss and emptiness on the mahamudra path, one is free from all concepts. In the sutrayana, or sutra path, there are no externals involved, whereas the tantrayana resorts to abhishekas and the like. In the sutra path, you practice shamatha and vipashyana according to the mahamudra, whereas in the vajrayana path you practice utpatti- and sampannakrama.

S: It is said that one should rest in the freshness of the present moment of consciousness, but when I sit down to meditate I don't experience any freshness at all.

R: Mahamudra might sound extremely easy, but it is actually quite difficult to practice. The extraordinary means of the vajrayana, or the utpatti- and sampannakrama, are used precisely because it is so difficult to achieve realization directly. For instance, the six yogas of Naropa are a means of recognizing the nature of mind and mahamudra is practiced in connection with these yogas. It is also very helpful for one's practice to strengthen bodhichitta and devotion.

S: What is meant by the phrase "transmitting the blessings of realization"?

R: It refers to the blessings that are transmitted through the Kagyü lineage. The Kagyü or mahamudra lineage is described as the lineage of realization and of ultimate meaning because in the golden chain of transmission of the Kagyüs the inspiration of the ultimate meaning is transmitted from guru to disciple.

S: In order to actualize bodhichitta, the desire to remain in samsara until all beings have attained buddhahood, does one have to remain in samsara until all beings have become buddhas?

R: If someone genuinely feels this way and is not merely paying lip service to the idea or trying to contrive it, this in itself speeds up his or her own realization of buddhahood. This is the "trick" in the mahayana. However, one cannot deliberately use bodhichitta as a trick, since the desire to lead all beings to enlightenment must be genuine and unfabricated. One will then be able to progress quite rapidly along the path and achieve either enlightenment or the higher bodhisattva bhumis for the benefit of beings. Only then is one really able to lead all beings to buddhahood.

S: How can one judge one's own meditation experiences?
R: The best way is to ask a teacher in whom you have trust.

S: Also, how can one be sure that one is adopting the proper view?
R: This is precisely why it is so important to have a spiritual friend on the path.

S: But we have so little contact with our teachers.
R: At the beginning it is important to relate to a teacher in order to be sure that one has understood the instructions and that one can carry them out and practice them properly. However, after that, it is not necessary to always be with one's teacher; it is enough to meet him occasionally. The situation in India and Tibet was originally quite similar to the one in the West.

S: What is the meaning of threefold purity?

R: It is being free from certain concepts that we have. For instance, when we give somebody something, we have a notion of a gift, of ourselves as the giver, and of the other person as the receiver. Being free from these conceptual obscurations means recognizing that neither giver, receiver, nor gift have actual existence, that they are not separate from one another. This applies not only to the paramita of generosity, but also to all the others, since only in connection with supreme knowledge or prajña do the first five paramitas become actual means of liberation.

S: What is the meaning of the line "unborn is the nature of birth"?

R: We have to go back to the previous line, "mere appearance is the vividness of the trikaya," which refers to the ultimate nature of all things. Their nature is emptiness, or rather they are devoid of true existence, thus they are the dharmakaya. Based on emptiness, everything arises unobstructedly—this is the sambhogakaya. This unobstructedness manifests in many ways as nirmanakaya. Thus, all three kayas are present in phenomena.

"Unborn is the nature of birth" refers to the dharmakaya aspect, since ultimately there is no true arising or birth. Since emptiness means unobstructed potential, everything appears unobstructedly. This is birth, even though ultimately nothing is born. In this way, the unborn is endless; between these two dwelling is not really possible. The nature of birth is unborn—this is the dharmakaya. The unobstructedness is the sambhogakaya, and the manifold manifestations are the nirmanakaya.

S: What is the difference between sambhogakaya and nirmanakaya?

R: The unobstructedness of our minds expresses itself as the sambhogakaya and its myriad manifestations are the nirmanakaya. The main difference lies in subtle versus coarse manifestation. Sambhogakaya can only be experienced by beings on higher, purer levels, whereas the nirmanakaya can also be experienced by those on impure levels.

S: What is the difference between dharmadhatu and svabhavikakaya?

R: The svabhavikakaya is the unity of the trikaya, and this is also true for the dharmadhatu. Dharmadhatu refers to the space of phenomena, their emptiness or dharmakaya, whereas the svabhavikakaya refers to the unity of the three kayas. Dharmadhatu and svabhavikakaya are merely two terms to designate the same thing.

S: If thoughts come up while one is practicing shamatha meditation with form, should one look into their nature?

R: No. In shamatha meditation with form one should only strive to notice the thoughts that arise; without either suppressing or following them, one should return to one's concentration.

S: Are the three types of shamatha practiced in a single session?

R: No, they are practiced one after the other, starting with the easier forms.

S: Could you briefly describe the difference between shamatha and vipashyana?

R: Shamatha is basically a form of concentration, whereas vipashyana is investigating with discriminating awareness wisdom. For instance, shamatha might involve focusing un-distractedly on the breath, whereas vipashyana would be examining the nature of the breath. If you are meditating on a yidam, shamatha involves concentrating on the form of the yidam, whereas vipashyana is awareness of the yidam's appearance, attributes, and so forth. It is highly recom-mended to alternate between these two aspects, first focus-ing by means of shamatha, and then applying awareness or vipashyana, and then again focusing, and so on.

S: Should one practice shamatha meditation before doing one's ngöndro practice?

R: The actual practice of the path of mahamudra involves doing the preliminary practices or ngöndro first, and then practicing mahamudra shamatha and vipashyana in a situa-tion like the three-year retreat. However, there is nothing wrong with practicing shamatha before doing ngöndro. It might actually be easier to visualize the refuge tree in this way. It all depends on the teacher's style, on which aspect he decides to highlight.

S: At the end of the mandala offering it says that one makes outer, inner, secret, and absolute offerings to one's teacher. What does this mean?

R: Outer offerings are material, for instance the mandala offering itself. Inner offerings involve offering up one's body, speech, and mind. Secret and absolute offerings in-volve offering emptiness and threefold purity.

S: To what extent is sampannakrama like vipashyana?

R: Vipashyana is recognizing ultimate truth, the empti-ness of all phenomena, on the basis of mental stillness. The completion stage of vajrayana, or sampannakrama, involves progressively dissolving into luminosity the visualization one has constructed and recognizing the emptiness of everything. By their very nature, phenomena are emptiness; they are devoid of true existence. We recognize this through vipashyana and sampannakrama—so on one level it is actually the same.

S: I have often heard it said that vipashyana is the fruition of shamatha. Why should one then practice vipashyana separately from shamatha?

R: In general, vipashyana is the fruition of shamatha. This means that based on mental stillness one can see the actual reality of all phenomena. But it is difficult to accomplish this with shamatha alone. For this reason it is useful to integrate vipashyana into one's shamatha practice by practicing both aspects in alternation. In this way shamatha meditation reinforces vipashyana insight, which in turn strengthens shamatha meditation.

S: What is the difference between the realms of form and the formless realms?

R: Both are god realms. In the form realms one experiences a subtle physical body, whereas the formless realms are purely mental states. They involve experiencing concentration on "limitless awareness," "limitless space," and so on, without the concept of a body.

S: How can practitioners with children find the time to practice?

R: If both parents are Buddhists, then each can set aside a particular time for his or her practice—one can practice for one or two hours in the morning, and the other for the same amount of time in the evening. It is important to schedule as much time as possible for one's dharma practice. Meditation is a habit one acquires; the point is to cultivate that particular habit. Habits are also the cause for our wandering in samsara, because we have negative habitual tendencies in our minds. The effect of meditation is to weaken these habitual tendencies, and in order to meditate it is important to be regular in order to create a new habit. It is more helpful to practice regularly, if only for small periods of time, than to practice intensively once in a while. In addition to regular practice, one should also try to do retreats occasionally.

S: Are the four yogas actualized on the bodhisattva bhumis?

R: The relationship between the bodhisattva bhumis, the five paths, and the four yogas is as follows: The path of union, the second of the two paths, is subdivided into four phases, one of which is patience. This corresponds to the first yoga, one-pointedness. The path of insight, the third path, corresponds to the second yoga, simplicity. With this realization one reaches the first bodhisattva bhumi. The fourth path, the path of meditation, corresponds to the third yoga, one taste. On this path one attains the so-called impure (first to seventh) and pure (eighth to tenth) bhumis. The fifth path, the path of no more learning, corresponds to the fourth yoga, nonmeditation, and to the eleventh bhumi, or buddhahood.

S: Could you please explain mahamudra action once again?

R: The thing to stress most of all is discipline of body and speech and also behavior in accordance with the bodhisattva path of the six paramitas. As long as one has not completely recognized the nature of mind it is important to lead a disciplined life in terms of one's body, speech, and mind, and also to develop the desire to benefit others and to practice the six paramitas. Once one has realized the nature of mind, then everything becomes right action, as in the case of the siddhas, since there is no longer any difference between good deeds to be cultivated and bad deeds to be avoided.

However, at our level, these are merely lofty words that apply only to those who have already attained high levels of realization. A person who has not attained this realization but acts as if he had is committing a big mistake. If one has no realization and observes forms of behavior in one's teacher that are possible only with that realization, one could get the wrong idea and start behaving in a similar way oneself even though realization is lacking. At that point one would be overwhelmed by one's own conflicting emotions.

S: What is the meaning of the line: "Cast mind-made knowledge far away"?

R: Nobody can practice mahamudra without preparation. It is necessary to follow the path step by step. This is why one first practices ngöndro, and then yidam meditations with corresponding mantra recitations, and so forth. These aspects of the path gradually liberate one from dualistic notions. Through ngöndro and yidam meditations, impure appearances can gradually be brought to a pure level until eventually one is able to practice a truly uncontrived form of meditation. Only at that point can one apply the line: "Cast mind-made knowledge far away." Nobody can do this at the beginning.

S: Should one nevertheless keep in mind the goal of becoming a mahasiddha?

R: Yes, one should. However, it is not enough to think that one would eventually like to reach that stage. The aspiration in itself is fine, but one should know what is involved. There is a quote from Sakya Pandita which says: "If you practice mahamudra like a simpleton, this is the cause for rebirth as an animal." Practicing like a simpleton means practicing without the proper view. In order to have good meditation practice, it is essential to know the ground, view, and path, for example, quite well. Otherwise, if one simply sits down to meditate with ones's eyes wide open without having the faintest clue of what mahamudra is all about, this will only lead one to the animal realms. Sakya Pandita wrote an entire book on the effects of this type of mistake in one's meditation practice.

There is no path that is deeper and more direct than that of mahamudra and maha ati. There is no other path that leads to the ultimate goal—all other approaches eventually flow into this one. However, in order to practice the path, we have to follow it step by step, because we are too caught up in our dualistic confused notions.

In this regard, there is a proverb that says: "If you practice maha ati in the evening, you will attain enlightenment that same night; if you practice it in the morning, you will attain enlightenment that morning. If you practice mahamudra, you will attain enlightenment in an instant." There is no deeper path. All that one needs is to be well prepared, otherwise one will not be able to practice the path properly and will miss one's goal.

S: Isn't there a danger that an intellectual approach could affect our progress in mahamudra meditation?

R: Not at all, since thoughts and concepts do not affect mind—they are mind. On the mahamudra path they dissolve into themselves. Thoughts and mind are not different from each other. Once one has understood the nature of mind one can see that thoughts and mind are one. One experiences thoughts as being self-liberated; this is the experience of dharmakaya.

Appendixes

......

1

A Brief Biography of His Eminence Jamgön Kongtrül Rinpoche

by Bokar Tülku Rinpoche

......

NAMO GURU MATI DHARMA SINGHA YE.
The true nature of the vajra realm is unchanging and
  permanent,
Yet in order to train disciples,
You display inconceivable, miraculous illusions,
Such as the appearance of birth and death; I bow to you.
Your wondrous nirmanakaya, complete with all the marks
  of the Buddha,
Rests in meditation like a sun in the space of luminosity.
At this time I have composed the mere seed of a biography
To inspire the faith of myself and others.

Jamgön Kongtrül Lodrö Thaye was one of the most brilliant
stars in the galaxy of scholars and siddhas from Tibet, the
land of snow. Predicted by the Buddha, he was the crown
jewel in the *rime* (nonsectarian) movement of Buddhism in
Tibet. He was born on December 14, 1813, to Sönamphel
and Tashitso in front of Mount Pema Lhatse, one of the eight
sacred places in Kham (Eastern Tibet). Lodrö Thaye be-

came learned in the ten ordinary and extraordinary branches of knowledge, and it became his responsibility to explain and compose texts, which incorporated a great number of teachings from both the old and new traditions, including the lineages of oral teachings, hidden treasures (terma), and teachings of pure vision. These were all brought together in Lodrö Thaye's great Five Treasuries of Knowledge. Like a second Buddha, he served all traditions of dharma without any bias, through his teaching, practice, and activity. At the age of eighty-seven on January 19, 1899, he passed away.

In the garden of Samdrup Chöling at Dowolung Tshurphu, the unexcelled heart center of the dakinis, the second Jamgön Kongtrül, Kyentse Öser, was born in 1902 as the son of the fifteenth Karmapa, Khakhyap Dorje, of whom he was the heart son as well. He studied, mastered, and practiced to perfection the treatises of the sutras and tantras in general, and in particular, the Five Treasuries, the path of liberation, which focuses on the mahamudra as it is elucidated in the special teachings of the Kamtsang Kagyü. Khyentse Öser attained realization of the ultimate lineage and became the lineage holder of the sixteenth Gyalwang Karmapa. Many times over, he gave teachings, empowerments, and reading transmissions from the old and new traditions, such as the Rinchen Terdzö, and he rebuilt the retreat center of Tsatra Rinchen Drak (his residence at Palpung Monastery), supplying it with everything needed. He passed away on the tenth of May 1952, having accomplished great deeds for the benefit of the teachings and sentient beings.

The name of the third Kongtrül incarnation is Jamgön Kongtrül, Karma Lodrö Chökyi Senge, perfect guide of unequaled kindness, whose aspirations, activity, and accomplishments for the precious dharma and sentient beings in

general, and the Kagyü lineage in particular, have been a
wondrous light in these dark times. For this reason, his name
is spoken with great reverence. As his last testament, the
previous Jamgön Kongtrül, Khyentse Öser, stated that his
reincarnation would be in central Tibet and that the house-
hold, parents, and time would be predicted by the Gyalwang Karmapa. Accordingly, in a first letter of recognition,
the sixteenth Gyalwang Karmapa wrote the following
prophecy:

> In the central part of the country, surrounded by snow
>   mountains,
> With the father's name De and the mother's Pema,
> From a wealthy family of pure ancestry,
> A boy of the wood horse year with excellent signs
> Is without any doubt Jamgön, the incarnation of Lotsawa
>   Vairochana.
> Raising the victory banner of the teachings,
> He will give life to all Buddhist traditions
> And especially to the lineage of Gampopa.

According to this vajra prophecy Jamgön Kongtrül Rinpoche was born on the first of October 1954, the male horse
year of the sixteenth cycle, in Lhasa, from whence the Dalai
Lama guided the spiritual and temporal life of Tibet. His
father was Tsering Topgyal of Sadutshang, a prominent family, and his mother was Pema Yudrön, the daughter of Sa-
wang Ngawang Jigme Ngabo, a cabinet minister in the Tibetan government. Before and after his birth, many
wonderful signs appeared to his mother, and he was recognized without any doubt as the reincarnation of Jamgön
Kongtrül by His Holiness the Dalai Lama and the Gyalwang
Karmapa through the vision of their stainless wisdom.

Under their direction, Yönten Phüntsok, the Treasurer of

the former Jamgön Kongtrül Rinpoche, repeatedly requested the Sadutshang family to entrust the *tülku* to his *labrang* (monastic organization). At last they consented, and when he was one year and five months old, Jamgön Kongtrül Rinpoche was formally recognized and offered robes and his title. At the age of six, he was enthroned by His Holiness the Gyalwang Karmapa at the old monastery in Rumtek, Sikkim. From then onward, Jamgön Kongtrül Rinpoche as a heart son was inseparable from His Holiness, who supervised his education right from the very beginning, starting with reading, writing, and memorizing texts. At the age of thirteen, he received from His Holiness the sixteenth Karmapa getsul ordination along with Shamar Rinpoche and Tai Situ Rinpoche, on the fifteenth day of Saga Dawa (the fourth Tibetan month) of the male fire horse year at Rumtek's Karma Shedrup Chökhor Ling (Dharma Chakra Center). At that time, he received the name Jamgön Kongtrül, Karma Lodrö Chökyi Senge, Tenpe Gocha Ngedön Gyurme Trinle Künkhyap Palzangpo.

Jamgön Kongtrül Rinpoche then studied a great number of texts, both in general and specifically, with Khenchen Thrangu Rinpoche, a great scholar and holder of the vinaya. His further studies also included all the tantras of Marpa's tradition, especially those of the Karma Kamtsang, and the lama dances, preparation of mandalas, chanting, and musical instruments pertaining to the practices of Padmasambhava, Vajrakilaya, and others. Jamgön Kongtrül Rinpoche received from Khyabje Kalu Rinpoche, master siddha and the activity emanation of Jamgön Kongtrül Lodrö Thaye, teachings ranging from the mahamudra preliminary practices of the Kamtsang tradition up to empowerments, reading transmissions, and explanations for Gyalwa Gyamtso, Demchok, Dorje Phakmo, and especially, the Six Yogas of

Naropa, Mahamudra, the Five Golden Teachings of the Shangpa Kagyü, the great empowerments of Kalachakra and Rinchen Terdzö, and at different times, countless other teachings of the new and old traditions.

At the age of twenty, on the fifteenth day of the first month (the month of miracles) in the female water ox year, he received full gelong ordination at the Dharma Chakra Centre from his Holiness the sixteenth Gyalwang Karmapa, who acted as the khenpo (abbot) for the occasion, since he is master of the qualities of discipline and learning, well versed in the pitakas, the second Shakyamuni of this degenerate time, and leader of all those who hold ordination. Jamgön Kongtrül Rinpoche took gelong vows along with Chamgön Situ Rinpoche and Khyabje Gyaltsap Rinpoche, and was assisted by a master of procedure and other monks to complete the necessary number. Believing them to be the very foundation of the dharma, Jamgön Kongtrül Rinpoche always guarded carefully these precious vinaya rules, protecting them as if they were his own eyes. He gave the ordinations of getsül and gelong to about three thousand monks in India, Nepal, and Tibet, both the worlds of East and West, and so became a great holder of the vinaya.

From His Holiness the Gyalwang Karmapa, Jamgön Kongtrül Rinpoche received the bodhisattva vows, which are the foundation of the mahayana path, from the traditions of both Nagarjuna and Asanga. He continually practiced the many aspects of a bodhisattva's path—the six paramitas, the four ways of gathering disciples, and so forth—training in the extensive activity of the bodhisattva, and manifesting as a great one himself.

Jamgön Kongtrül Rinpoche had great faith, respect, and devotion for his spiritual teachers, the source of all paths and practice, and received from them many teachings of the sutra and tantra traditions. Especially, his relationship to the Gyalwang Karmapa, embodiment of all refuges, was one of total devotion, respect, and pure vision, which were greater than even that for the Buddha himself. Rinpoche served His Holiness perfectly and received from him all the profound oral instructions, such as the Five Great Treasuries, all the empowerments, reading transmissions, and explanations of the Kamtsang Kagyü, the Root Text of Mahamudra, and so forth. In particular, the realization of mahamudra, which is the heart blessing of the ultimate lineage, was transferred to him and he became a great siddha.

In 1976 and 1980, Jamgön Kongtrül Rinpoche accompanied the Gyalwang Karmapa on a tour of numerous places in America, Europe, and Southeast Asia. After His Holiness' parinirvana, Jamgön Rinpoche continued to travel to Europe and Asia, and established branches of the Rigpe Dorje Foundation in many countries and the Paramita Charitable Trust in India, to further his activities of social development for the benefit of others. Through empowerments, explanations, and advice, he generously gave teachings for three different types of students in accordance with their needs, and so became like the medicine that restored the teachings and healed sentient beings.

In 1983, in order to counteract obstacles to the swift return of His Holiness the Karmapa, Jamgön Rinpoche built a Sidok Stupa with the proper measurements, mantras, dharanis, and consecration. For the same reason, he initiated the practice of 100 million recitations of the Vajrasattva mantra every year on the occasion of Saga Dawa (the fourth Tibetan month). In 1984, following the wishes of His Holiness, he started the construction of a new building for Karma Shri Nalanda Institute and it was inaugurated in June of 1987. Not only did Jamgön Kongtrül Rinpoche provide for all the furnishings of the entire building, including the statues and so forth for the shrine hall, but he also found the means to support about 150 students, comprised of many tülkus, lamas, and monks.

Jamgön Rinpoche visited Tibet in 1984, gave empowerment and teachings at Palpung Monastery to a vast gathering of monks and lay people, and ordained about 500 monks, giving them getsül and gelong vows. He then visited Lhasa and Tshurphu Monastery (the Seat of His Holiness the Gyalwang Karmapa) where he gave empowerments and teachings to monks and lay people, and the ordinations of getsül and gelong to about one hundred. Furthermore, he was able to obtain permission for the reconstruction of Tshurphu, toward which he donated all the offerings that were made to him during his journey.

In 1988, Rinpoche constructed a new monastery at Lava near Kalimpong, West Bengal, and presently about 108 monks reside there, ten of whom are involved in a three-year retreat following the tradition of the golden dharma in the Shangpa Kagyü. Likewise, in 1988 he started the construction of Phullahari Retreat Center in Nepal, where there are now about fifteen monks practicing. In 1990, he gave the great Kalachakra empowerment to the monks and lay people of Rumtek and donated funds to initiate the conducting of the Kalachakra puja there on an annual basis.

In 1991, Jamgön Kongtrül Rinpoche returned to Tibet and visited Derge Gönchen where he gave an empowerment, reconsecrated the old and new Derge Printing House, and made donations to them. Thereafter, he journeyed to Palpung Monastery and gave the great Kalachakra initiation to about 550 tülkus and lamas of the area, including Sangye Tendzin of Japa Gönshap Surmang Tentrül, Dodrak Tülku, and many others, and further, there was a crowd of about 10,000 lay people. He also gave getsül and gelong ordinations to about 550 people. Next he traveled to Damkar Monastery in Nangchen, where he again gave the Kalachakra empowerment to about 10,000 sangha members, including lamas and tülkus, such as Shangu Tülku, Kyodrak Tendzin, Salga, Drukpa Tülku, Demon Tülku, and many others.

In February of 1992, he gave the Kagyü Ngakdzö empowerments to the monks, nuns, and lay people of Rumtek, and to numerous sangha members from the East and West. He also inaugurated the new building of Karma Jamyang Khang, a primary school for monks, for which he had arranged funding and participated in the design and construction. As his last activity, Jamgön Kongtrül Rinpoche offered mantras and dharanis to fill the new statue of the Buddha in the main shrine hall of Rumtek monastery. Due to his pure samaya with His Holiness, he was able to cover the entire statue with gold. Once he had consecrated the statue, Jamgön Rinpoche told his attendants, "Now I have fulfilled the wishes of His Holiness."

In brief, to Jamgön Rinpoche one can say as in this quote:

I pray to you, source of all qualities, the one rich in faith, discipline, learning, generosity, intelligence, modesty, and humility.

From childhood, he naturally had all the qualities of a noble being. His faith and pure vision of his teachers was unparalleled, and especially, his devotion to his root lama, Vajradhara Gyalwang Karmapa, was fully equal to that of all the previous lineage holders of the Kagyü tradition. From the time His Holiness became ill, until he dissolved his mind into the dharmadhatu, Jamgön Kongtrül Rinpoche was not separate from him for even one moment. He was never tired nor careless for a moment in attending to the physical needs or following the commands and wishes of his lama. With great respect he served His Holiness even to the point of cleaning His Holiness' personal bathroom and sweeping his floors when it was necessary. His life is a teaching to people like us who tend to treat the dharma and the lamas like water by the roadside, which we take when we need it, but do not respect or give devotion from our heart.

Jamgön Rinpoche studied numerous sutras, tantras, their commentaries and oral instructions, from traditions in particular and in general. As a sign of having genuinely realized these teachings, he displayed the qualities of faith, pure vision, loving-kindness, and genuine concern for the well-being of others, qualities that were so much a part of him that they became inseparable from his name. He constantly fulfilled the wishes of others through giving away all that was offered him to build monasteries, to establish centers of learning and practice, to create representations of the Buddha's body, speech, and mind, and to support the sangha and the poor and needy.

With clear wisdom of the world and of dharma, he soothed the mental sufferings of others, cut through the net of their doubts, and guided them onto the right path through direct and indirect means. To his attendants and all those, high or low, with whom he related, Jamgön Rinpoche always showed the qualities of constant friendship, modesty, humility, and gratitude; he perfected all these qualities that are esteemed in the world. We, his disciples, should always remember this perfect life story of our supreme guide and seek to emulate it with faith, respect, and pure vision.

At the age of thirty-nine (by the Tibetan calendar), Jamgön Kongtrül Rinpoche suddenly passed away, due to the obstacles for Buddhism and people in general, and in particular for the Kagyü tradition. Considering his age, learning, qualities, aspirations, and activities, his passing has been an unbearably sorrowful event for his disciples and all who knew him. Yet, as ordinary people with limited understanding and realization of how things truly are, we are unable to know the profound methods for benefitting sentient beings in the right time and place. We should, therefore, always look at his life with pure vision, great faith, and devotion, and try to attain in our lifetime the supreme achievement of mahamudra through receiving in our mindstream the blessing of his body, speech, and mind. We should always turn our minds toward praying that his perfect incarnation will swiftly return, and that his life and activities will be brought to perfection following the aspirations he has made of the Dharma and sentient beings.

> From now until enlightenment, supreme lama,
> May we always serve and rely on you.
> May we persevere in practice and complete the path,
> Giving up what is negative and perfecting the positive.

Following the request of Jamgön Rinpoche's attendants, Tenzin Dorjee and Sonam Chöphel, this was written at Rumtek Retreat Center, Yiwang Samten Chökhor Ling, on the 5th of May, 1992, by Bokar Tülku, Karma Ngedön Chökyi Lodrö, whose devotion is inspired by the life of Jamgön Lama. Sarva Mangalam. This translation was made by Ringu Tülku and Michele Martin in May of 1992, in Sikkim.

2

Supplication to the Kagyü Gurus

......

You who bind the secret joy,
Śri Heruka, I supplicate you.

In the charnel ground of the play of joy and light,
Wisdom ḍākinī consort, I supplicate you.

In the secret bhaga of the land of Uḍḍiyāṇa,
Glorious Buddha Tilopa, I supplicate you.

In the sphere of activity of the wisdom ḍākinī consort,
The mahāpaṇḍita, great siddha Nāropa, I supplicate you.

Surrounded by the assembly of Nairātmyā Devī,
Lord Lhotrakpa, father and son, I supplicate you.

Sporting with the queen in the celestial realm,
Lord repas, greater and lesser, I supplicate you.

Holder of the ultimate lineage, the sacred teaching of
     mahāmudrā,
Lord physician, uncle and nephews, I supplicate you.

Revealing the miracles of luminosity,
Lord Tüsum Khyenpa, I supplicate you.

Possessing the buddha activity which subjugates those
    difficult to tame,
Lord Sanggye Rechen, I supplicate you.

Possessing the mastery which overpowers the phenomenal
    world,
Lord great Pomtrakpa, I supplicate you.

In the east at Kaṃpo Kangra, holder of the Practice
    Lineage,
Lord Karmapa, I supplicate you.

You, the lord of mudrā messengers,
Lord Mahāsiddha, I supplicate you.

Expanding the stream of blissful wisdom,
Lord Rangjung Dorje, I supplicate you.

In the clear palace of the luminous vajra,
Victorious Yungtön Shikpo, I supplicate you.

Samaya holder of the unified maṇḍala of the devas,
Lord Rölpe Dorje, I supplicate you.

The poet who sings songs of great blazing passion,
Lord Khachö Wangpo, I supplicate you.

You who wear the crown of glorious, invincible yoga,
Lord Teshin Shekpa, I supplicate you.

Enjoying the great taste of mind, bliss, and prāṇa,
Lord Chöpal Yeshe, I supplicate you.

Spreading the bindu of the great wrathful one,
Lord Ratnabhadra, I supplicate you.

You whose roar of bliss pervades the sky,
Lord Thongwa Tönden, I supplicate you.

Greatly intoxicated by the joy of Mañjuśrī,
Lord Pengar Künkhyen, I supplicate you.

You who promote profound brilliant realization,
Great Lord Goshri, I supplicate you.

You who achieved the siddhi of taste with the gaze of
simplicity,
Lord Chötrak Gyatso, I supplicate you.

You whose mind has perfected the aspects of supreme
union,
Lord Sanggye Nyenpa, I supplicate you.

You who fully reveal yourself to your son-disciples,
Lord Mikyö Dorje, I supplicate you.

Bestowing bliss on sentient beings pervading space,
Glorious Könchok Yenlak, I supplicate you.

You, the nirmāṇakāya endowed with a compassionate
heart,
Lord Wangchuk Dorje, I supplicate you.

From the palace of prāṇa purified in the avadhūti,
Lord Chökyi Wangchuk, I supplicate you.

On the uṣṇīṣa of the brahmarandhra,
Lord Chöying Dorje, I supplicate you.

In the profound, brilliant, divine palace,
Lord Trakpa Chokyang, I supplicate you.

In the palace of space and wisdom,
Glorious Yeshe Nyingpo, I supplicate you.

In the divine dome of Potala,
Lord Yeshe Dorje, I supplicate you.

Marvelous with profound and brilliant knowledge,
Lord Chökyi Töntrup, I supplicate you.

Supreme, fearless, accomplishing the benefit of all,
Lord Changchup Dorje, I supplicate you.

Spreading the sunlight of the teachings of the two
knowledges,
Lord Chökyi Jungne, I supplicate you.

Perpetually enjoying the gaṇacakra of great bliss,
Lord Düdül Dorje, I supplicate you.

You who know the illusory character of the whole
phenomenal world,
Lord Chötrup Gyatso, I supplicate you.

From the palace of the dharmakāya of unchanging truth,
Lord Padma Nyinche, I supplicate you.

You can establish whoever encounters you in
nonreturning,
Lord Thekchok Dorje, I supplicate you.

Illusory musician of supreme bliss and emptiness,
Lord Lodrö Thaye, I supplicate you.

Whoever hears your name is led to the path of liberation,
Lord Khakhyap Dorje, I supplicate you.

Glorious conqueror of the hordes of the four māras,
Lord Padma Wangchok, I supplicate you.

You who liberate those poisoned with the ignorance of
dualistic fixation,
Lord Jamgön Guru, I supplicate you.

May I be liberated from the sophistries of the two truths of
   dharma.
In the nakedness of true ordinary mind,
Which is the penetrating path of abandoning hope and
   fear,
May I realize buddha in the palm of my hand.

Glossary

......

abhisheka (wang) An empowerment ceremony in which the teacher introduces the student to the mandala of a given yidam and empowers him to meditate on that yidam. Besides the abhisheka, a reading transmission (lung), and an oral explanation (thri), are also necessary to effectively practice the vajrayana.

alaya-vijñana (künzhi namper shepa) The consciousness that is the ground of everything. The aspect of mind that constitutes the basis for confusedly identifying with a self and dualistic thinking.

Atisha (982–1054) Also known as Dipamkara Shri Jñana. A meditation master and scholar at the Buddhist University Vikramashila in India. After being repeatedly invited to teach in Tibet, he accepted and contributed greatly to establishing the Buddhist teachings there. His student Dromtönpa is the founder of the Kadampa school.

bardo (lit. "in-between state") In general usage refers to the state between death and rebirth. In actual fact, there are six bardos: the bardo of life, sleep, meditation, death, dharmata, and becoming.

bhumi (sa) One of the ten stages on the path of a bodhisattva.

bindu *See* prana, nadi, bindu.

bodhichitta (changchup-kyi sem) A mental attitude oriented toward attaining enlightenment in order to benefit all beings.

Bodhichitta is divided into two aspects: relative and ultimate. Relative bodhichitta is both the aspiration to attain enlightenment for the benefit of others and the practical application of this aspiration through the practice of liberating behavior in the form of the paramitas. Ultimate bodhichitta involves realizing the inseparability of emptiness and compassion.

bodhisattva (changechup sempa)   A person who works tirelessly to achieve enlightenment for the benefit of all sentient beings, without ever feeling discouraged. In the narrow sense, the term refers to someone who has realized emptiness and developed compassion. In the broad sense, it includes anyone who has taken the bodhisattva vow, a ceremony in which one promises to achieve buddhahood for the benefit of others.

Bön   A shamanistic religion that was practiced in Tibet before the spread of Buddhism.

Bönpo   Practitioner of Bön.

cloudy mind (kleshamanas; nyönmongpe yid)   The seventh consciousness, an aspect of mind that rests on the alaya-vijñana, that experiences confusion, and that has the concept of a self.

dakini (khandroma, lit. "sky-walker")   Dakinis represent inspirational impulses of awareness that help the practitioner in his quest for wisdom. They appear in friendly, semi-wrathful, and wrathful forms. Some dakinis are yidams, while others are types of energy that protect the teachings and the practitioner. There are also some who do not benefit beings.

dependent origination (pratityasamutpada; tenching drelwar jungwa)   The pattern of cause and effect in one's experience of life situations, with phenomena arising interdependently, based on a variety of causes and conditions.

dharma (chö)   In this book the term should be taken to mean Buddhist teachings, except in the expression "eight worldly dharmas."

dharmadhatu (chöying)   The space of phenomena; ultimate reality.

dharmakaya *See* kaya.

dharmapala (chökyong) *See* three roots.

dharma robes The three robes of a monk or nun.

eight transmission lineages (eight lines of transmission) Nyingma, Kadampa, Kagyü, Sakya, Shangpa, Shije, Orgyenpa, and Jonangpa. A distinction is made between the "old" and "new" traditions. The old tradition is the Nyingma, that arose during the first spread of Buddhism in Tibet in the eighth century, as opposed to the new traditions, that came to Tibet during the second wave of translations of Indian Buddhist texts. This phase begins with the translator Rinchen Sangpo (958–1051).

eight worldly dharmas Four pairs of opposites that rule our lives as long as we struggle to achieve the first set and reject the second. These are gain and loss, joy and pain, fame and obscurity, praise and blame.

enlightenment Buddhahood. The Tibetan word for Buddha, *sanggye,* is made up of two syllables that illustrate the two aspects of buddhahood. *Sang* means "completely purified," that is, purified of all obscurations, including the sleep of ignorance. *Gye* means "completely developed" and refers to the development of all qualities and wisdom. Enlightenment or buddhahood is a state of complete purity and wisdom.

five paths A description of spiritual development in the mahayana outlined by: path of accumulation, path of union, path of meditation, path of insight, and path of no more learning. With the path of insight, one achieves the first of the ten bodhisattva bhumis. Within the bhumis, a distinction is made between the so-called "impure" bhumis, the first seven, and "pure" bhumis, the eighth, ninth, and tenth. The eleventh bhumi is the realization of complete enlightenment, corresponding to the path of no more learning.

formless realm (zukme kham) *See* three realms of samsara.

form kayas (zuk ku) *See* kaya.

four dharmas of Gampopa A short text by Gampopa:

> May my mind be one with the dharma,
> May my practice progress along the path,
> May the path clarify confusion,
> May confusion dawn as wisdom.

four extremes Existence, nonexistence, both existence and nonexistence, neither existence nor nonexistence. These are four false notions that may arise when one reflects on reality, and that are countered by madhyamaka.

four great and eight lesser lineages (schools) *See* Kagyü.

four ordinary and four special preliminaries *See* ngöndro.

four noble truths (denpa zhi) The first teachings of Buddha Shakyamuni: suffering, the cause of suffering, the cessation of suffering, and the path leading to the cessation of suffering.

four yogas Four stages of the path of mahamudra: one-pointedness, one taste, simplicity, and nonmeditation. Each of these four is divided into three levels of realization.

Gampopa (1079–1153) Main student of Milarepa and teacher of the first Karmapa, Tüsum Khyenpa. Gampopa blended together two traditions: the Kadampa lineage of Atisha and the mahamudra lineage transmitted to him by Milarepa. At Taklha Gampo he founded the first Kagyü monastery in Tibet. Gampopa is the source of the four great and eight lesser lineages (schools) of the Kagyü lineage. He is also known as Takpo Lharje, the physician from Takpo.

garuda (khyung) An ancient Indian mythological bird that hatches full-grown from the egg and thus symbolizes the awakened state of mind.

ghanta *See* vajra.

giving and taking (tong len) A form of meditation derived originally from the Kadampa tradition, aimed at developing bodhichitta and training the mind.

guru (lama) *See* three roots.

guruyoga (lame naljor)   A form of meditation through which one realizes that one's own mind is inseparable from the mind of the teacher and from ultimate reality, that is, enlightenment.

Hevajra (Kye Dorje)   One of the five main yidams of the Kagyü school. Hevajra was one of Marpa's yidams.

incarnation(trülku)   Someone who through spiritual realization has attained the ability to manifest deliberately in the world for the benefit of other beings.

Jewel Ornament of Liberation (Takpo Thargyen)   One of Gampopa's most important texts. It is one of the texts most used by Kagyü teachers to present the gradual path of the mahayana.

Kadampa   Name of a tradition that was transmitted by Atisha's students. Although it has not survived as a separate school, it was absorbed into and transmitted by the other lineages of Tibetan Buddhism.

Kagyü   One of the four main lineages of Tibetan Buddhism, the other three being the Nyingma, Sakya, and Gelukpa. After Gampopa, the Kagyü lineage was also called Takpo Kagyü. The Kagyü lineage is divided into the so-called four great and eight lesser lineages. The four great lineages date back to Gampopa's main students:

1. the Karma Kagyü (or Kamtsang Kagyü) school, founded by the first Karmapa, Tüsum Khyenpa
2. the Phakdru Kagyü, founded by Phakmo Drupa
3. the Tsalpa Kagyü, founded by Öngom Tsültrim Nyingpo and his student Zhang Darma Drak
4. the Barom Kagyü, founded by Barom Darma Wangchuk

   The eight lesser lineages can be traced back to the eight main students of Phakmo Drupa. They are the Drikung, Taklung, Yamtseng, Thropu, Shuksep, Yelpa, Martsang, and Drukpa. The only surviving schools are the Karma Kagyü among the four great lineages and the Drukpa, Drikung, and Taklung among the eight lesser.

kalpa   An inconceivably long span of time; an eon.

karma (le)   The inevitability of cause and effect that conditions the different types of existential experience. Mental impressions left by actions, words, or thoughts leading to the experience of suffering are called negative karma, whereas those which lead to the experience of happiness are called positive karma.

Karma Kagyü   *See* Kagyü.

Karmapa   As spiritual Head of the Kagyü lineage, the Karmapas embody all buddha activity. This is expressed in the name itself, since *karma* means "activity." The first Karmapa, Tüsum Khyenpa (1110–1193) was Gampopa's main disciple. Before his death, he left behind a letter explaining the precise circumstances of his next rebirth. In accordance with his description, the second Karmapa, Karma Pakshi (1206–1283) was born deliberately as an incarnation of the first. He was the first incarnation to be recognized in Tibetan history. Since that time, the Kagyü lineage has been transmitted by the Karmapas, with each successive Karmapa leaving behind specific instructions concerning his next incarnation.

karuna (nyingje)   The quality of the bodhisattva which involves extending kindness toward all sentient beings without distinction.

kaya (ku)   Enlightenment body. Dharmakaya (chö ku) is the state of buddhahood itself; it is the nature of mind, or emptiness, and is meaningful for oneself. The two form kayas, the sambhogakaya (long ku) and nirmanakaya (trül ku) manifest out of compassion for the benefit of beings and are meaningful for others. Sambhogakaya buddhas such as Vajrasattva can only be experienced directly by realized bodhisattvas, whereas nirmanakayas such as Shakyamuni Buddha manifest as humans and can be perceived by beings with no particular realization. The unity of the three kayas is called the svabhavikakaya (ngowonyi-kyi ku).

lineage   A succession of Buddhist teachers who transmit a particular tradition.

lineage supplication   A supplication to the Takpo Kagyü transmission lineage that describes mahamudra in concise form.
Composed by Jampal Zangpo, disciple of the sixth Karmapa
and teacher of the seventh.

lower realms   The hell, hungry ghost, and animal realms. *See*
three realms of samsara.

madhyamaka (uma)   Philosophy taught by the Buddha with regard to the nature of emptiness, the ultimate mode of existence
of all things. These teachings of Buddha were later commented
on by Indian teachers like Nagarjuna, Chandrakirti, and others
and constitute the philosophical foundation for the vajrayana.

maha ati (dzokpa chenpo, dzokchen)   The "great perfection."
Similar to the mahamudra of the Kagyü tradition, it is transmitted mainly by the Nyingma school. In their nature and purpose, mahamudra and maha ati are the same, although the
methods and the path differ.

mahamudra (chakgya chenpo)   The "great seal" or great symbol
of reality. A distinction is made between ground, path, and
fruition mahamudra. Ground mahamudra concerns the nature
of mind and the proper view, path mahamudra the application
of mahamudra meditation, and fruition mahamudra the realization of the nature of mind.

Mahamudra Supplication   A prayer by the third Karmapa,
Rangjung Dorje, describing the nature of mind.

mahasiddha (drupchen)   A practitioner of the vajrayana who
has attained all the ordinary and extraordinary siddhis. *See* siddhi.

mahapandita   An Indian title given to highly accomplished
scholars.

mahayana   *See* yana.

Maitripa (eleventh century)   Also called Maitri. Indian mahasiddha from whom Marpa received the mahamudra transmission.

mandala (khyil khor)   The term has several meanings: It refers:
(a) to the spiritual force-field of the buddhas; (b) to the utterly

beautiful universe full of previous objects that one visualizes mentally in order to offer it to the buddhas in the mandala offering; and (c) to the round disk on which this universe is constructed symbolically.

mantra (sang ngak)   Words or syllables used in vajrayana meditations.

mantrayana   Vajrayana. *See* yana.

Mara   Difficulties and obstacles due to confusion, false views about reality, and wrong behavior.

Marpa (1012–1097)   The "Great Translator," considered an emanation of Hevajra. Marpa traveled three times from Tibet to India in order to receive teachings from his main gurus Naropa and Maitripa. He was the first Tibetan lineage holder of the Kagyü school and Milarepa's guru.

merit (sönam)   *See* two accumulations.

Milarepa (1040–1123)   An important teacher of the Kagyü school who attained complete enlightenment in one lifetime. He is also called the greatest of yogis. Milarepa was Gampopa's guru.

nadi   *See* prana, nadi, bindu.

Naropa (1016–1100)   Also called Naro. An Indian mahasiddha, disciple of Tilopa and Marpa's guru.

ngöndro   Preliminary practices for the path of mahamudra. A distinction is made between the four ordinary and the four special preliminaries. The ordinary preliminaries are the four reminders: precious human birth; impermanence; karma; and suffering of samsara. The special preliminaries are: refuge and bodhichitta, vajrasattva meditation; mandala offering; and guruyoga.

nine techniques of shamatha   Experiences on the path of shamatha meditation are presented in nine points in the commentaries. They are: resting the mind, continuous resting, renewed resting, precise resting, disciplining, calming, calming completely, one-pointedness, and evenly resting. The pith instructions describe the development of mental calmness in five stages, which are illustrated through five images: a waterfall, a mountain torrent in a narrow gorge, a broad, slowly flowing river, a calm ocean, and a butter lamp in a room with no drafts.

nirmanakaya *See* kaya.

nirvana (nyangde) State of liberation from the circle of rebirths. Often used as a synonym for enlightenment.

obscurations Everything that prevents one from realizing buddhahood, the nature of one's mind.

paramita (paröl-tu chinpa) The six paramitas or liberating actions are the essence of the mahayana: generosity, discipline, patience, exertion, meditation, and prajña. According to some systems, there are four additional paramitas: skillful means, aspiration, strength, and wisdom.

path of causes and characteristics (gyu tsen nyi thekpa) Another name for the sutra path. In order to recognize emptiness, the characteristic, one practices the path, thus accumulating merit for enlightenment. *See also* yana.

path of liberation *See* path of skillful means.

path of insight *See* five paths.

path of skillful means (thap lam) Although all yanas contain skillful means for attaining realization, the vajrayana is specifically called the path of skillful means or upayayana because of its wealth of powerful techniques. Within the vajrayana a distinction is made between meditations involving visualizations, which are the path of skillful means, and meditations without such visualizations, which are the path of liberation (dröl lam).

prajña (sherap) The sixth paramita, transcendent knowledge. Only through prajña do the first five paramitas become instruments of liberation. *Prajñaparamita* is the realization that reality is beyond the duality of being versus nonbeing. Since it is this realization that leads to enlightenment, prajñaparamita is often called the "mother of all the buddhas" and represented as a female buddha.

prana, nadi, bindu (tsa, lung, thikle)   On the vajrayana path of skillful means one meditates on the nadis or different pathways of energy in one's body, the energy winds or prana which circulate through them, and the bindus or essential components of the body. This type of meditation belongs to the special skillful means of the vajrayana.

Literally, the term bindu means "drop;" and describes the essence or pith of something. In shamatha meditation, the bindus are sometimes used as an "essential" support for concentration in the form of tiny visualized spheres. In the human body, bindu is the quintessence of maleness or femaleness through which life arises.

pratyekabuddha (rang sanggye)   A state of liberation from samsara. Those who endeavor to achieve this state have the following characteristics: they fear samsara, strive for nirvana, have little compassion, are proud, keep their teacher secret, and long for solitude. Their path consists mainly in meditating on the twelve links of dependent origination. *See also* yana.

reality   A distinction is made between relative and ultimate levels of reality. Relative reality is the world of one's experience, based on dependent origination. Ultimate reality is emptiness, the true unconditioned nature of things. These two aspects of reality or levels of truth are inseparable from each other.

realm of desire (dö kham)   *See* three realms of samsara.

realm of form (zuk kham)   *See* three realms of samsara.

refuge (kyap dro)   Taking refuge involves the decision to integrate the three gems into one's life. One takes refuge in the Buddha as an example of one who has attained the goal, in the dharma or teachings as the path, and in the sangha or community of practitioners as helpers on the way. In addition, in the vajrayana one takes refuge in the three roots.

refuge tree   A way of depicting the three gems and three roots, visualized during prostations. *See* ngöndro.

Rinpoche (lit., "precious one")   A Tibetan title and form of address for a realized Buddhist teacher.

Sakya Pandita (1181–1251)   Title of Künga Gyaltsen, one of the most important teachers of the Sakya school.

samadhi (ting nge dzin)   State of mental absorption.

sambhogakaya   *See* kaya.

sampannakrama   *See* utpattikrama and sampannakrama.

samsara (khorwa)   A state of ignorance characterized by suffering, in which one experiences a continuous round of rebirths.

sangha (gendün)   Community of Buddhist practitioners.

sevenfold service   A type of prayer for accumulating merit, consisting of seven sections: prostrating, offering, confessing, rejoicing, requesting to teach, asking to remain, and dedicating the merit for the benefit of beings.

shamatha (shine)   A form of meditation that involves dwelling in mental peace.

Shepa dorje   "Laughing Vajra," name given to Milarepa by his teacher Marpa. *See* Milarepa.

shravaka (nyen thö)   A state of liberation from samsara. Those who endeavor to achieve this state have the following characteristics: they are afraid of samsara, strive after nirvana, and have little compassion. Their path mainly involves meditating on the four noble truths and their sixteen subdivisions. *See also* yana.

siddha (drupthop)   *See* mahasiddha.

siddhi (ngödrup)   Special abilities developed through meditation. A distinction is made between general siddhis and the ultimate siddhi. General siddhis are extraordinary physical and mental abilities, whereas the ultimate siddhi is the realization of the nature of mind, that is, emptiness.

six consciousnesses   The five sense consciousnesses and mind-consciousness.

six dharmas of Naropa (Naro chö druk)   Six intensive meditation practices, sometimes called the six yogas, that have been handed down mainly through the Kagyü lineage: inner heat (tummo), illusion body (gyulü), dreaming (milam), luminosity (ösel), ejection of consciousness (phowa), and in-between state (bardo). The goal of these practices is to realize the nature of mind. Naropa received them from various teachers and passed them on to his student Marpa.

skandha (pungpo) The five skandhas are the aggregates of which an individual and his experiences are made up. These are form, feeling, perception/impulse, formation, and consciousness. As long as one is in a state of confusion, one believes that one of the skandhas or all of them are real. However, if one looks into them, one cannot find an ego either in an individual skandha, in all five, or outside the skandhas.

sugatagarbha Buddha-nature, the potential for enlightenment inherent in every being.

sutra (do) Buddha's teachings can be divided broadly into the sutrayana and the tantrayana. The sutrayana comprises all the hinayana and mahayana teachings, and the tantrayana refers to the vajrayana. *See also* yana.

sutrayana *See* yana.

svabhavikakaya *See* kaya.

tathagata (deshin shekpa) "One who has gone to suchness"; a name given to buddhas.

Takpo buddha *See* Kagyü Lineage.

tantrayana *See* yana.

ten bhumis *See* five paths.

ten directions The four cardinal directions, the four intermediate directions, plus zenith, and nadir. Can also mean "beyond all directions."

three gems (könchok sum) Buddha, dharma (teachings of the Buddha), and sangha (community of practitioners). *See also* refuge.

three realms of samsara (kham sum) The desire realm, the form realm, and the formless realm. To the realm of desire belong the hell, hungry ghost, animal, human, jealous god, and "lower" god realms; in these realms, the senses are the most important element of one's existential experience. The other two realms correspond to the "higher" levels of the god realms. In the form realm, one still experiences the illusion of a subtle body, as opposed to the formless realm which is purely mental.

three roots (tsawa sum) Guru, yidam, and dharmapalas; an expanded form of refuge in the vajrayana. The guru is the source of inspiration and enables one to experience the nature of one's own mind. The yidams are the source of siddhis. Although these sambhogakaya forms—subtle manifestations of dharmakaya—are only experienced by realized bodhisattvas, in the vajrayana they are visualized as objects of meditation. As meditational deities, the yidams embody the practitioner's enlightened nature. The dharmapalas are also sambhogakaya forms. They are the source of actions and protect the practitioner from obstacles along the way to buddhahood. Both yidams and dharmapalas are in their essence inseparable from the guru.

three times (tü sum) Past, present, and future.

three-year retreat A traditional form of retreat which lasts three years, three months, and three days.

Tilopa (988–1069) Also called Tilo. Indian mahasiddha and one of the forefathers of the Kagyü lineage. He was Naropa's guru.

transcendent knowledge *See prajña.*

two accumulations The accumulation of merit (sönam-kyi tsok), that is, of positive impressions in the mind, and the accumulation of wisdom (yeshe-kyi tsok), that is, insight into the nature of things.

Uddiyana (Orgyen) The pure land of the dakinis, the dwelling place of Tilopa.

utpattikrama and sampannakrama (kye rim, dzok rim) In the vajrayana path of skillful means, a distinction is made between two stages in meditation practice: the utpattikrama or development stage of stabilizing a particular visualization, and the sampannakrama or completion stage of dissolving the visualization into emptiness.

vajra and ghanta Two of the most important ritual implements in the vajrayana. The vajra (dorje) symbolizes indestructibility and compassion and is always held in the right hand. The bell or ghanta (drilbu) symbolizes supreme knowledge and is held in the left.

Vajradhara (Dorje chang) The enlightened state, or dharmakaya, in sambhogakaya form. *See* kaya.

Vajrasattva (Dorje Sempa) Buddhahood in sambhogakaya form, expressing the purifying force of enlightenment. *See* kaya.

vajrayana (dorje thekpa) Another name for the tantrayana. *See also* yana.

Victorious One (Gyalwa) Name given to buddhas who have conquered all illusion.

vipashyana (lhakthong) Clear awareness, clear insight into the nature of mind.

visualization Meditation technique used in the vajrayana which consists, for instance, in imagining a yidam.

vows Three types of vows are distinguished: outer, inner, and secret. Outer vows involve a form of discipline through which one avoids harming othes. They are called the vows of individual liberation and consist of seven or eight subsets of vows, for monks, nuns, lay householders, and so on. The inner vow is the bodhisattva vow. Secret vows are tantric vows of the vajrayana.

wisdom (yeshe) *See* two accumulations.

yana (thekpa) Although the literal meaning is "vehicle," it is applied to the Buddhist path. Three yanas are distinguished in Buddhism: the shravakayana, the pratyekabuddhayana, and the bodhisattvayana. The first two belong to the so-called hinayana (thek men) or "small vehicle." Briefly stated, the main feature of these two yanas is that practitioners strive mainly for individual liberation.

The third yana, or bodhisattvayana, is the so-called maha-yana (thek chen) or "large vehicle." Briefly stated, the practi-tioner of this yana strives to attain enlightenment through com-passion and wisdom for the benefit of all beings. Thus, his responsibility is far greater than in the hinayana. Mahayana can be subdivided into sutrayana and tantrayana, both of which lead toward the same goal. However, in the tantrayana, the practitioner has access to highly effective means for developing compassion and wisdom and transforming impurity to purity. Vajrayana and mantrayana are synonyms for tantrayana.

yidam *See* three roots.

yogin, yogini (naljorpa, naljorma) Male and female practition-ers of the vajrayana.